FRESH MIDWEST

FRESH MIDWEST

Modern Recipes from the Heartland

MAREN ELLINGBOE KING

Photographs by
Maren Ellingboe King & Eliesa Johnson

Countryman Press

An Imprint of W. W. Norton & Company
Independent Publishers Since 1923

For information about permission to reproduce selections from this book, write to
Permissions, Countryman Press, 500 Fifth Avenue, New York, NY 10110

For information about special discounts for bulk purchases, please contact
W. W. Norton Special Sales at specialsales@wwnorton.com or 800-233-4830

Manufacturing by Toppan Leefung Pte. Ltd.
Book design by Allison Chi
Production manager: Devon Zahn

Countryman Press
www.countrymanpress.com

An imprint of W. W. Norton & Company, Inc.
500 Fifth Avenue, New York, NY 10110
www.wwnorton.com

978-1-68268-696-6

10 9 8 7 6 5 4 3 2 1

To Dashiell and Ari

CONTENTS

chopped onion
chicken broth   1/3 c. flour
salt   1/3 c. milk
                       4 c. milk

...hine cabbage, celery, onion
...broth, salt, caraway seed in
...covered saucepan

Wild Rice Soup
5 slices, chopped bacon & onion
                    saute'
...beef browned
...crm. of mushroom so...
...ked wild rice
...broth, till desir...

cookin' Ready to Eat Pickles Serves
Recipe from the kitchen of Home Ex.
        7 c. sliced cucs
        1 c. green pepper
        1 c. onion sliced
        2 tbsp salt
        1 "   celery seed

Lefse
8 c. mashed potatoes (riced)
. c. cream
. c. butter (margarine)
1 tb. salt (scant).
3-4 c. fleur
   Cook potatoes. Mash with cream,
butter, and salt. Ceol. Mix in
flour. Roll thin on fleured beard
er cloth. Bake on grill 400.

LEFSE
1 qt. warm mashed potatoes
2 tbsp. butter
3 tbsp. milk or cream
1 tsp. salt
½ c. sugar
. c. sifted flour
Mash potatoes with butter
d milk or cream...

Corn Relish
18 ears corn
1 small cabbage
3 green papers   } Chop
4 good sized onions   )
¼ c salt
2 c sugar
2 tbsp ground mustard
1 qt vinegar

...pkt. of dry yeast
...about its equivalent in
...this in warm (not hot) water and
...until it foams up.
...margarine or butter

Ripe Tomato Relish
1 pk ripe tomatoes
        chopped & drained
        finely chopped
                4 red pepper
                4 green
                1 c. horse...
                seed

...Frances
...Crust White Bread
...dry yeast
...water

Deiligt Flatbrød
2 cups flour
3/4 tsp. salt
t cup lard or veg. shorteni...
1 cup boiling water

Mix flour, salt, and shorten...
r pie crust. Add boiling water...
e into a roll...
ll out into c...
wheat or regu...
in. Cut circ...
cookie she...
t brown

Rhubarb
5 cups - cubed
3 c sugar
Set in Ref. over...
in morning 1 min -
orange slices c...

Doughnut   Caroline
2 c buttermilk } m...
3 c sugar

Chicken (grandma)
Roll in butter - crumbs (cornflakes)
Put in pan to bake
our can of mushroom
Bake 350°
gravy

Chocolate Cake Dessert Good
Lillian
Bake loose Duncan Hines cake mix
in 2 pans - to make layers
when baked slice thru middle
and fill with whipt whipped 3 P.
1 tbsp cocoa + sugar

INTRODUCTION

When you think of Minnesota, you probably think of cold winters and nice people.

You might also think of hotdish, the unofficial state dish, or possibly a mayonnaise-laden "salad" or Jell-O mold. You probably don't think of a state that's become a hotbed of diverse cuisine in recent years, from Hmong to Somali to Mexican.

The food I grew up on was straight out of the Midwestern comfort food canon, including dishes like glazed ham and creamed corn for Easter brunch, and Swedish meatballs and mashed potatoes on Christmas Eve. This book features those simple, comforting dishes but also draws inspiration from the increasingly diverse population in Minnesota and modern Scandinavian cooking. If you're not familiar with the cuisine of the region brought over by Scandinavian immigrants in the nineteenth century, it's food that is simple yet hearty, inspired by the long, dark winters and humid summers filled with lightning bugs and bursting tomato plants.

I grew up on a 5-acre hobby farm east of St. Paul, in a suburb called Woodbury, but my ancestors were farmers across southern Minnesota and Wisconsin. Many eventually settled in a small town south of the Twin Cities called Lakeville, where both of my parents grew up.

Most of my extended family is still located in the surrounding suburbs, and my husband, Ari, and I moved back to Minneapolis in 2020. Ari is an Oakland, California, native, raised by a Jewish mother and Black bull rider father—so needless to say, moving to the Midwest has been a new experience for him (not to mention that hotdish, layered salads, and Jell-O are all unfamiliar territory).

Many of the recipes in this book are based on archives I inherited from my grandmothers and great-grandmothers: Veola, Nancy, Judith, and Eleanor. My great-grandmother Judith Soberg kept hundreds of recipes, mostly written on index cards, scribbled on the backs of scratch paper, or clipped from the newspaper. Some have notes like "Good" or "from Ida," and many are vague in both ingredient amounts and directions. (For example, one piecrust recipe simply reads: "½ cup lard, 1½ cups flour, 6 T. water, baking powder, salt." No directions of any kind.) Through the process of making these recipes, I acted as translator into the modern era, and I learned more about women who I knew very little about—my grandma Judith died when I was three, and most of the women she

CLOCKWISE FROM TOP LEFT:

My grandma Veola Ellingboe, great-grandma Judith Soberg, and great-great grandma Hilda Sundal.

My newly married parents (Lynn and Randy Ellingboe) in the early 1980s, pictured with the traditional Norwegian almond ring cake, kransekake.

My grandpa Oscar Ellingboe in the kitchen of their house in Lakeville, Minnesota.

Scenes of typical farm life found in my family's archives.

exchanged recipes with were friends or family who passed away long before I was born. But while rolling out her recipe for sugar cookies, I could picture them sitting in their farmhouse kitchens, gossiping over a cup of strong coffee and a plate of these same cookies.

The recipes in these archives were not complicated, and true to new conveniences of the 1940s and '50s, many used time-saving ingredients such as cream of mushroom soup, prepared Pillsbury dough, or canned vegetables. When it came to food, the Midwestern women of the early and mid-twentieth century were usually not looking to innovate or, honestly, even to necessarily be all that flavorful. Rather, they needed to feed their husbands and children something hearty to sustain them throughout the long days of fall harvest and long, cold winter nights. While fresh produce was available all summer, it was often more

practical than artisanal—an inexpensive way to feed the family—and preserving fruits and vegetables was how they kept the meals coming during the winter months when nothing else was available.

This book draws on these recipes, but it updates them with modern techniques and ingredients. The way I eat now has a lot more fresh produce, more herbs, more spice and heat and acid than the sometimes-bland dishes of my childhood, and these recipes reflect that. While living in California from 2015 to 2020, I had access to an incredible array of fruits and vegetables, a far cry from the canned green beans and corn that was typical for my parents and grandparents during their childhoods. (My mother would also like me to point out that canned vegetables are strictly banned in her kitchen.) Though these recipes don't use processed ingredients, the dishes retain their nos-

talgic taste, and are no less simple to prepare. This book is a mix of those "taste memories," as my dad calls them, and new recipes inspired by my heritage and years spent living on the coasts.

These recipes also draw on my Scandinavian heritage—Minnesota is home to the largest population of Norwegians and Swedes outside of Scandinavia, and my family is nearly all Norwegian and Swedish in origin—and the incredible bounty of local produce available across the Midwest, especially in summer and fall. And of course, this wouldn't be a Minnesotan cookbook without at least a few recipes for hotdish, a one-pot casserole that traditionally consists of meat, a vegetable, a starch, and canned cream of mushroom soup. You won't find canned cream soups or vegetables in these recipes (though you will find frozen tater tots—like Heinz ketchup, it's an ingredient that's impossi-

ble to improve upon at home). Some recipes call for Scandinavian ingredients such as lingonberries, caraway seeds, and juniper berries, which may not be familiar to home cooks outside of the Midwest (but are luckily now widely available online).

I wrote and took the photographs for this book in 2021, just a few months after moving back home to Minnesota after a decade spent in New York and California—and during a year when the entire world was still grappling with the isolation, death, and changes that the coronavirus pandemic brought to our lives. Instead of trips to New York to meet with my editor, there were Zoom meetings. Instead of large family gatherings to share recipes in progress, there were bags of food left on front steps. Instead of a two-week photo shoot with a full crew, there was mostly me, alone, taking photos in my kitchen and living room. I also found out

I was pregnant with our first child just a few weeks after signing my contract, and our son grew as the number of recipes I tested swelled from 10 to 20 to 100. I turned in my manuscript just a couple of weeks before his due date, effectively giving birth to both of my first babies within days of each other.

The coronavirus pandemic has taken away so much from us, but there were moments of growth and joy as well. My husband, Ari, and I had already decided to leave the Bay Area for Minnesota before the pandemic began, but the ways that COVID-19 changed our society only emphasized those reasons: cost of living, traffic, being closer to family. I don't think this would have been the same book if I had written it while living in California. Making my grandma Veola's Swedish Meatballs (page 139) with mashed potatoes on a hot July day was not exactly in line with the season, but taking one bite made it feel like Christmas. (In my family, we always have Swedish meatballs, mashed potatoes, lefse, and lutefisk on Christmas Eve.)

The seasons changed from winter to spring to summer to fall as my belly grew, and I combed through recipe cards and cooked seemingly endless rounds of hotdish, baked goods, and pickles. As I did all this, I came to know my grandmothers, and the women in their communities who shared their recipes, in an entirely new way. Before I began working on this book, I can't say I made hotdish very frequently, and my weeknight dinner repertoire was more often inspired by South Asian or Italian dishes instead of my native state—but preparing these recipes brought me closer to my newly re-embraced Midwestern roots in a deeper way than even moving to Minneapolis has done.

This book is not about meal prepping, or shortcuts to get dinner ready in 15 minutes. Rather, it is about feeding your family, whether that includes one other person or a group of 12.

Most of the dishes are designed for four to six people to share. Few take longer than an hour of cooking time—because who has time to shop, cook, and do everything else that's on your plate in the precious few hours between work and sleep?

For those occasions when you do have all day to cook, I suggest you refer to the Gatherings chapter. It highlights four "feasts" that reflect larger parties, one for each season. The Maple-Glazed Ham Buffet Menu (page 185) with its homemade rolls and a bevy of side dishes is evocative of the epic Thanksgiving buffet my parents host each year, complete

"This book is a mix of those 'taste memories,' and new recipes inspired by my heritage and years spent living on the coasts."

with a ham and two turkeys. The Smorgasbord Brunch Menu (page 167) for the spring season is inspired by my dad's traditional birthday breakfast: a spread of cheese, sausage, pickled and smoked fish, rye bread, and hard-boiled eggs to create smørrebrød, Danish open-faced sandwiches. The Norwegian Fondue Party Menu (page 159) features a fondue made with Jarlsberg cheese (similar to Swiss cheese, and a staple in my parents' refrigerator) and calls to mind my extended family's old-school tradition of fondue on New Year's Eve. Finally, the Midsummer Kräftskiva Menu (page 177) combines the disparate yet related midsummer crawfish boils in Sweden and the American South—and its main ingredient (crawfish) is found in ponds and lakes across Minnesota.

Until recently, Midwestern cookbooks have mostly been limited to compendiums of church recipes, or they've focused on homestead cooking. Authors like Amy Thielen, Molly Yeh, and Beth Dooley have long been working to bring the foods of the Midwest to a wider audience, and my hope is that this book will expand on their efforts. Of course, a vast array of other excellent cooks are also bringing new meaning to the term "Midwestern cuisine," dishes that come from beyond the Northern European immigrants of my ancestry. Just to name a few, in the Twin Cities alone we have Ann Kim slinging Korean-influenced pizzas and more, Yia Vang bringing Hmong specialties to a wider audience, and Sean Sherman drawing on local, native plants to create dishes inspired by the indigenous people of the region. However, there is also a dearth of books featuring the unique combination of traditional, comforting, cream- and butter-heavy recipes of the early twentieth-century Midwest, their Scandinavian influences, and fresh, unprocessed ingredients. That's what I'm aiming to do with this book.

I'd like to see Midwestern food achieve the same status that Southern food has in recent years, showcasing an array of diverse recipes across an entire region, with hundreds of variations. I want to capture those familiar dishes of my childhood—the recipes of Scandinavian immigrants, of busy mothers, of farmers' families—and bring them to a wider audience, because they are dishes worth preserving and celebrating. Although my recipes use fresh produce, not canned, and homemade béchamel instead of cream of mushroom soup, the meaning behind the dishes is the same: This is food that's meant to be shared with the people you love.

BREAKFAST & BRUNCH

When you wake up to -10° temperatures on a cold January morning, a warm cup of coffee and hearty breakfast is essential.

On those cold days, I like to start with some easy but flavorful eggs and toast, such as the Smoked Salmon Scrambled Eggs (page 5). They come together in 10 minutes but evoke memories of one of my favorite restaurant dishes, and ensure a good start to the day.

In contrast to the busy workweek, Saturday morning brunch was always an occasion when I was growing up. After working long hours all week, my mother as a theater teacher and my father as a civil engineer, my parents usually began the day with a cup of coffee and glass of juice, followed by something special: tender scones, omelets, or Belgian waffles with crispy bacon. If my sisters and I had any say in the matter, we requested Mickey Mouse pancakes drizzled in plenty of my dad's homemade maple syrup. It was a perfect way to transition from the frazzled weekdays to the weekend, even if it was followed shortly afterward by chores and the tasks that inevitably piled up around the house.

These days, Ari and I often do the same on Saturdays or Sundays: He'll cook bacon while I scoop pancakes onto the griddle, or pull loaves of steaming Brown Butter Zucchini Bread (page 16) out of the oven. Even though we both work from home most of the time, there's something about lingering over breakfast on the weekends that feels special, a way to make the most of our limited weekend hours.

The recipes in this chapter run the gamut from easy to complicated, from ready in minutes (Wild Rice Pancakes, page 25) to a multiday affair (Cardamom Coffee Buns, page 19). However, much of the preparation for the more complicated recipes can be done ahead of time, so your Almond Kringle (page 10) or Banana Caramel Rolls (page 13) can be popped in the oven the morning you plan to serve them (and it's worth planning ahead to do so)—then all you need to do is pull up a chair, pour yourself an extra cup of coffee, and linger over the newspaper or a good book.

Smoked Salmon Scrambled Eggs   5

Egg & Mushroom Hotdish   6

Mashed Potato Pancakes   8

Pumpkin Bread   9

Almond Kringle   10

Banana Caramel Rolls   13

Brown Butter Zucchini Bread   16

Cardamom Coffee Buns   19

Old-Fashioned Buttermilk Doughnuts   23

Wild Rice Pancakes   25

Smoked Salmon Scrambled Eggs

Serves 4

This easy breakfast is inspired by a favorite restaurant in New York City called Buttermilk Channel. I'm generally not a brunch person (at restaurants at least—at home bring on all the brunch foods!), but when my husband and I lived in Brooklyn, we would often walk down to the Carroll Gardens neighborhood on a Saturday morning and sit at the bar. I would almost always order their perfectly scrambled eggs with smoked salmon and cream cheese, served with toast and hash browns.

8 eggs

1/3 cup half-and-half or whole milk

1 teaspoon kosher salt, plus more if needed

1/2 teaspoon ground pepper, plus more if needed

2 tablespoons butter

6 green onions, chopped, white and green parts separated

4 ounces hot smoked salmon, broken into pieces

4 ounces cream cheese, cut into 1/2-inch pieces

Hearty toasted bread for serving

DIRECTIONS

1. Vigorously whisk the eggs, half-and-half, salt, and pepper together in a medium bowl.

2. Melt the butter in a large skillet over medium-low heat. Add the white parts of the green onions and cook for 1 minute. Pour in the eggs and cook, stirring frequently, until the eggs are just beginning to set, about 2 minutes.

3. When the eggs are almost done cooking, stir in the salmon. Scatter the cream cheese pieces over the eggs. Add the remaining green onions and cook until the cream cheese begins to melt, about 30 seconds.

4. Season with more salt and pepper if needed, and serve immediately with buttered toast.

Egg & Mushroom Hotdish

Serves 8 to 10

Inspired by my grandma Nancy, who made a similar brunch dish to feed a crew of hungry grandkids, this savory hotdish (you can call it a strata or egg bake if that's more your style) is everything I want for a crowd-pleasing egg dish. It can be made ahead and customized to your taste, and it's bursting with umami flavor. Even my sister Annelise—who usually doesn't like mushrooms!—is a fan.

4 tablespoons butter, plus more for pan

1 pound fresh cremini or baby bella mushrooms, thinly sliced

1 large shallot, minced

2 tablespoons all-purpose flour

3 cups half-and-half

1½ teaspoons kosher salt

1 teaspoon ground pepper

1 tablespoon fresh thyme leaves

½ loaf country style or sourdough bread, torn into 1-inch pieces (about 4 cups)

5 ounces (about 1¼ cup) grated Jarlsberg, Gruyère, or Swiss cheese

10 eggs

4 slices bacon, cooked and chopped into pieces (optional)

¼ cup minced chives

DIRECTIONS

1. Preheat oven to 350°F. Butter a 9-by-13-inch baking dish or spray with cooking spray.

2. Melt 2 tablespoons of the butter in a large skillet over medium heat. Add the mushrooms and shallots, working in batches if needed. Cook until the mushrooms are browned, 5 to 10 minutes.

3. Add the remaining 2 tablespoons butter and the flour to the pan and cook until the flour is browned and nutty, about 3 minutes. Add 1 cup of the half-and-half and stir until combined. Season with 1 teaspoon of the salt and ½ teaspoon of the pepper and simmer until the sauce has thickened, about 5 minutes. Stir in the thyme.

4. Transfer the mushroom mixture to a large bowl. Add the bread pieces and cheese and stir until well coated. Spread the mixture in the prepared pan.

5. Whisk the eggs, remaining 2 cups half-and-half and remaining ½ teaspoon salt and pepper together in a large bowl. Pour the eggs over the bread mixture in the pan. Sprinkle the crumbled bacon over the top, if using. If making ahead, cover and refrigerate for up to 1 day.

6. Bake for 45 to 60 minutes, until browned and the center is set. If baking after refrigerating, bake for 60 to 70 minutes.

7. Sprinkle chives over the hotdish, cut into squares, and serve.

Mashed Potato Pancakes

Makes about 20

We make latkes every year for Hanukkah, and these potato pancakes come from the same idea. They are also a great way to use up leftover mashed potatoes. I like to eat these with sour cream and smoked fish, but they would also be delicious with bacon and eggs for breakfast (definitely not kosher), or even with homemade mayo (Homemade Mayonnaise, page 46) for a happy hour snack.

1 tablespoon vegetable oil, plus more for frying

1 small yellow onion, chopped

3 cups Garlic-Chive Mashed Potatoes (page 118) or mashed potatoes, chilled

2 eggs

¾ cup flour

½ teaspoon baking powder

Kosher salt to taste

Ground pepper to taste

DIRECTIONS

1. Preheat oven to 300°F. Heat 1 tablespoon oil in a large skillet over medium heat. Add the onions and cook until softened, about 8 minutes.

2. Place the onions, mashed potatoes, eggs, flour, and baking powder in a medium bowl. Stir to combine. Add salt and pepper to taste if needed.

3. Line a rimmed baking sheet with parchment paper. Form the mashed potato mixture into 2-inch balls. Place the balls on the prepared baking sheet. Chill for 30 minutes.

4. Pour vegetable oil into the skillet until it's about ¼-inch deep. Heat the oil over medium heat until very hot but not smoking.

5. Add three or four potato balls at a time, smashing each with a spatula to form a pancake. Fry until golden brown and crispy, 2 to 3 minutes per side. Remove to a rimmed baking sheet and repeat with remaining pancakes. Keep warm in the oven until ready to serve.

Pumpkin Bread

Makes one 8-by-4-inch loaf

I can't get behind the pumpkin spice craze that seems to take over come fall, but a classic pumpkin bread with my morning cappuccino? Yes, please. This easy quick bread comes from my grandma Veola, and is a must-bake once the air turns crisp in October. It's super moist thanks to a mixture of pumpkin puree, oil, and buttermilk. The mix of warming spices adds depth without becoming overwhelming.

1 cup pureed pumpkin

2 eggs

½ cup vegetable or canola oil

½ cup buttermilk

1⅓ cups flour

1 cup sugar

½ cup maple syrup

1 teaspoon baking soda

¾ teaspoon kosher salt

½ teaspoon baking powder

½ teaspoon cinnamon

½ teaspoon ground cloves

½ teaspoon ground nutmeg

½ teaspoon ground ginger

DIRECTIONS

1. Preheat oven to 325°F. Use butter or baking spray to coat an 8-by-4-inch loaf pan and line with parchment paper so that the parchment hangs over the long sides of the pan.

2. Whisk together the pumpkin, eggs, oil, and buttermilk in a large bowl. Add the flour, sugar, maple syrup, baking soda, salt, baking powder, and spices. Whisk until completely combined.

3. Pour the batter into the loaf pan. Bake until a tester in the middle comes out clean, about 1 hour 20 minutes. Cool for 10 minutes on a rack, then remove bread from the pan.

Almond Kringle

Makes two 20-inch kringles

This recipe was originally found in a letter to my great-grandma Soberg from her niece Violet, and I love the thought of sharing recipes that way. Though Violet's recipe included a date filling, I substituted it for almond. The almond filling is delicious on its own, but these kringles would also be wonderful with some raspberry or apricot jam or Rhubarb Compote (page 114) spread over the sweetened almond paste. The lard in the dough adds wonderful flakiness, but if you can't find it or have vegetarians in your crowd, use 1 total cup chilled butter instead. These are especially lovely to make (and share!) around the holidays.

PASTRY DOUGH

One ¼-ounce package yeast (2¼ teaspoons)

½ cup lukewarm water

4 cups all-purpose flour, plus more for rolling

3 tablespoons sugar

1 teaspoon kosher salt

½ cup (1 stick) butter, chilled, cut into ½-inch pieces

½ cup leaf lard, chilled

3 egg yolks (reserve whites for filling and topping)

1 cup lukewarm milk

FILLING

2 egg whites

8 ounces almond paste

⅓ cup sugar

¼ cup (½ stick) butter, room temperature

1 teaspoon lemon juice

1 teaspoon almond extract

½ teaspoon kosher salt

ICING & TOPPING

2 cups powdered sugar

3 to 4 tablespoons heavy cream

1 tablespoon butter, melted

1 teaspoon almond extract

¼ teaspoon kosher salt

2 cups sliced almonds

DIRECTIONS

1. **MAKE THE DOUGH:** Place the yeast and lukewarm water in a small bowl. Let stand for 10 minutes, until foamy.

2. Mix the flour, sugar, and salt in the bowl of a stand mixer. Add the butter and lard and use your fingers to combine into the flour mixture, squishing until the butter and lard are distributed throughout and form pea-size pieces. Attach the bowl to the mixer fitted with the dough hook.

3. Whisk the egg yolks and milk together in a glass measuring cup. Whisk into the yeast mixture, then add to the dough. Beat until the dough comes together and begins to pull away from the sides of the bowl, 2 to 3 minutes. Transfer to an oiled bowl, cover, and refrigerate for at least 8 hours or overnight.

4. **MAKE THE FILLING:** In the bowl of a stand mixer fitted with the whisk, beat 2 of the egg whites until soft peaks form, about 3 minutes.

CONTINUED ▶

5. Mix ¼ cup of the whipped egg whites, almond paste, sugar, butter, lemon juice, almond extract, and salt in a medium bowl until well combined. (This is easier with a mixer, but you can use a wooden spoon or whisk as well.) Set aside.

6. Lightly flour your work surface. Divide the refrigerated dough in half. Roll each piece into a 9-by-20-inch rectangle about ½ inch thick.

7. Divide the almond filling in half. Spread the filling down the middle of each piece of dough, about 3 inches wide. For each piece of dough, fold one-third of the dough over the filling. Spread the remaining whipped egg whites over the folded dough and down the other side. Fold the other side of the dough over the filling (dough will now be a 3-by-20-inch rectangle). Press the seams together and turn each dough over so the seam sides are down.

8. Line two rimmed baking sheets with parchment paper. Carefully transfer one kringle to each baking sheet. Form into a crescent or S-shape. Cover each with a towel. Let rise in a warm place for 2 hours.

9. Brush the tops of the dough crescents with egg white. Preheat oven to 400°F. Bake for 20 minutes, or until puffed and golden brown. Cool the kringles completely on a rack.

10. **MAKE THE ICING:** Whisk the powdered sugar, cream, butter, almond extract, and salt together in a small bowl.

11. Drizzle icing over the cooled kringles and sprinkle with almonds. Cut into slices and serve. Kringles can be stored, covered at room temperature, for up to 3 days.

Banana Caramel Rolls

Makes 12

The idea for these tender rolls was inspired by my grandma Nancy's Cabin Caramel Rolls, a dish she served every year at our family's annual Fourth of July gathering at my grandparents' northern Minnesota cabin when I was little.

Caramel rolls can be a little lackluster—the crumb too tough, the caramel too hardened, the rolls themselves lacking flavor. Enter: bananas. I love a good banana bread, and mashed bananas bring both tenderness and flavor to the brioche dough (thanks to my sister Solveig for the suggestion!). More sliced bananas are mixed with the filling and topping, resulting in tasty bites of caramelized fruit. For ease, I make these in a 9-by-13-inch baking dish. But we all know the crunchy edges are the best part—to maximize these, bake them in two round or square 9-inch pans, or even better, in extra-large muffin tins!

ROLLS

1½ cups whole milk or buttermilk, warmed to 110°F to 115°F

2 packets (4½ teaspoons) active dry yeast

½ cup sugar

2 eggs

6 cups all-purpose flour, plus more for rolling

2 teaspoons kosher salt

½ cup (1 stick) unsalted butter, room temperature

1 very ripe banana, mashed

CARAMEL & TOPPING

1½ cups brown sugar

¾ cup (1½ sticks) unsalted butter, softened

¼ cup corn syrup

1 teaspoon vanilla extract

¾ cup chopped pecans

3 bananas, cut into ½-inch-thick slices

Flaky sea salt, such as Maldon

FILLING

½ cup brown sugar

2 teaspoons cinnamon

Pinch of kosher salt

¼ cup (½ stick) unsalted butter, melted

DIRECTIONS

1. **MAKE THE ROLLS:** Combine the milk and yeast in the bowl of a stand mixer. Let sit until the yeast foams, about 10 minutes. Add the sugar and eggs and whisk until combined. Attach the bowl to the mixer fitted with the dough hook. Add the flour and salt and beat on low until a shaggy dough forms. With the mixer running on low, add the butter, one piece at a time. Increase the speed to medium and beat for 3 to 4 minutes, until the dough is smooth and begins to pull away from the side of the bowl. Beat in the mashed banana. The dough will still be soft and a bit sticky.

2. Transfer the dough to a lightly greased bowl and cover with plastic wrap. Let rise in a warm place for 1 to 2 hours, until doubled. Alternatively, refrigerate dough overnight.

3. Butter or coat a 9-by-13-inch pan with baking spray.

CONTINUED ▶

4. **MAKE THE CARAMEL:** While the dough rises, place the brown sugar, butter, corn syrup, and vanilla in a small saucepan. Melt over medium heat and bring to a simmer. Pour the caramel over the bottom of the prepared pan and sprinkle with pecans and half of the banana slices.

5. **MAKE THE FILLING:** Combine the brown sugar, cinnamon, and salt in a small bowl.

6. When the dough has risen, punch down in the bowl. Lightly dust a work surface with flour. Turn the dough onto the work surface and sprinkle with flour. Roll into a 12-by-18-inch rectangle. Brush the dough with ¼ cup melted butter, then sprinkle evenly with the sugar mixture and remaining banana slices. Starting on the long side, roll the dough tightly into a jelly roll. Use a sharp knife to cut into 12 equal pieces (each about 1 inch long). Evenly space the rolls apart in the pan over the bananas and pecans. Cover with a dish towel and let rise in a warm place until doubled, 30 minutes to 1 hour.

7. Preheat oven to 350°F. Bake the rolls for 35 to 45 minutes, until the rolls are well browned and cooked through, rotating the pan halfway through to ensure even browning. Line a rimmed baking sheet with parchment paper. Let the rolls cool on a rack for 5 minutes, then flip onto the prepared baking sheet.

8. Sprinkle with flaky salt and serve immediately. Alternatively, make up to 2 days ahead and store tightly covered at room temperature. Rewarm before serving.

Brown Butter Zucchini Bread

Makes two 9-by-5-inch loaves

My mother makes zucchini bread at least a few times every summer to make use of the massive crop from her garden. It's always been one of my favorite breakfast treats. I adapted this recipe from my great-grandma Soberg's version, using a 1:1 combination of browned butter and canola oil, adding more zucchini and cutting back a little on the cinnamon. Try olive oil instead of butter for a more savory flavor.

½ cup (1 stick) unsalted butter

3 eggs

½ cup vegetable oil

1 cup sugar

½ cup lightly packed brown sugar

3 cups grated zucchini (from about 2 medium or 1 large zucchini)

1 tablespoon vanilla

3 cups flour

2 teaspoons cinnamon

2 teaspoons baking soda

1 teaspoon kosher salt

½ teaspoon baking powder

DIRECTIONS

1. Melt the butter in a small saucepan over medium heat. Cook until the butter browns and smells nutty, swirling the pan every so often, 6 to 10 minutes. Set aside and cool for 15 to 30 minutes.

2. Preheat oven to 350°F. Coat two 9-by-5-inch loaf pans with baking spray and line with parchment paper so the paper hangs over the long sides of the pans.

3. Whisk the eggs in a large bowl until foamy, about 30 seconds. Add the reserved butter, oil, sugar, brown sugar, zucchini, and vanilla. Whisk well to combine. Sift the flour, cinnamon, baking soda, salt, and baking powder into the batter. Whisk until just combined and no dry spots remain.

4. Divide the batter between the loaf pans. Bake until the tops are golden brown and a tester inserted in the middle comes out clean, 45 to 60 minutes. Cool on a rack for 10 minutes before removing from pans.

5. To store, wrap the bread tightly in plastic wrap and store at room temperature for up to 1 week. Alternatively, freeze the baked bread for up to 2 months. Defrost overnight in the refrigerator before serving.

Cardamom Coffee Buns

Makes 12

Known as *kardemummabullar* in Swedish, these twisted pull-apart buns are served all over Scandinavia as part of *fika,* or the morning coffee break. Cardamom and coffee are a natural pairing, and I decided to amplify it even more by mixing instant espresso powder into the dough and filling. Though the buns are a daylong project with multiple rises and chilling periods, they're well worth the effort. To make the process easier, let the dough rise overnight in the refrigerator and finish the buns the day you plan to serve them.

COFFEE BUNS

1 cup whole milk

2¼ teaspoons active dry yeast
   (from one ¼-ounce packet)

3½ cups all-purpose flour, plus more for rolling

⅓ cup sugar

2 tablespoons ground cardamom

1 tablespoon instant espresso powder

1 teaspoon kosher salt

1 egg

6 tablespoons unsalted butter, room temperature

FILLING

½ cup (1 stick) unsalted butter, room temperature

½ cup brown sugar, packed

1 tablespoon ground cardamom

1 tablespoon instant espresso powder

TO FINISH

1 egg, lightly beaten

2 tablespoons sugar

2 teaspoons ground cardamom, preferably freshly
   ground from about 15 whole green pods

¼ cup maple syrup

DIRECTIONS

1. **PREPARE THE DOUGH:** Heat the milk in a small saucepan over medium heat to 110°F to 115°F. Transfer to a small bowl and whisk in the yeast. Let sit for 10 to 15 minutes, until foamy.

2. Place the flour, sugar, cardamom, espresso powder, and salt in the bowl of a stand mixer fitted with the dough hook. Whisk to combine. Beat in the milk mixture on medium speed. Add the egg and beat for 2 minutes, until the dough starts to come together. With the mixer running on medium, add the butter, 1 tablespoon at a time, beating after each addition. Beat until the dough pulls away from the sides of the bowl and becomes smooth and pliable, about 8 minutes.

3. Transfer the dough to a large buttered bowl. Tightly cover and rise until doubled in size, 1 to 1½ hours. When it's risen, punch down and tightly cover again. Refrigerate for at least 2 hours and up to overnight.

CONTINUED ▶

4. After the dough has chilled, lightly dust a large piece of parchment paper with flour. Roll the dough into a 12-by-16-inch rectangle. Transfer the dough on the parchment to a large rimmed baking sheet, cover with plastic wrap, and refrigerate for 1 hour.

5. **MAKE THE FILLING:** While the dough chills, combine the butter, brown sugar, cardamom, and espresso powder in a small bowl. Stir to make a rough paste. Line two rimmed baking sheets with parchment paper.

6. When the dough has chilled, transfer to your work surface. With the long edge facing you, spread the filling completely over the dough. Fold one short side one-third of the way to the middle, then fold the other side over that (like folding a letter). Roll the dough into a 12-by-14-inch rectangle. Trim any uneven edges as needed. With one of the folded sides at the top, use a sharp knife or pizza cutter to cut the dough into twelve 1-inch-thick strips.

7. Cut each strip down the middle, lengthwise, leaving about ¾ inch uncut at the top. Twist the dough strands around each other to form a spiral, then twist the dough into a circle, tucking the cut ends underneath. Repeat with the remaining strips. Transfer the buns to the prepared baking sheets. Cover with dish towels and let rise for 45 minutes to 1 hour.

8. **TO FINISH:** Preheat oven to 350°F. Brush each bun with the beaten egg. Bake until deep golden brown, 25 to 30 minutes, rotating the baking sheets halfway through.

9. While the buns are baking, mix the sugar and fresh cardamom in a small bowl.

10. Brush the warm buns with the maple syrup, then sprinkle liberally with the sugar mixture. Enjoy warm from the oven, or cool completely and store tightly covered for up to 5 days. Reheat for a few minutes in the oven before eating.

Old-Fashioned Buttermilk Doughnuts

Makes 24 to 28

This recipe was a challenge, I'm not going to lie. My great-grandma Soberg's recipe merely included the instructions "Add enough flour to make soft batter, drop with a doughnut maker" at the end of the preparation. Not being an experienced doughnut maker, I had no idea what the consistency of the dough should be like. The first batch was too thick, and the dough was lacking in flavor. The second was far too soft and was impossible to cut into any kind of shape, let alone lift out of the mixing bowl. But now I think I've found a happy medium, a subtly nutmeg- and vanilla-scented batter that tastes strongly of nostalgia: reminding me of the sugarcoated doughnuts served in a paper bag at state and county fairs all over the country.

3 cups flour, plus more for rolling
1 tablespoon baking powder
1 teaspoon kosher salt
½ teaspoon baking soda
¼ teaspoon nutmeg
¾ cup buttermilk
2 eggs
1 teaspoon vanilla paste or extract
2 tablespoons unsalted butter, room temperature
2 cups sugar
Vegetable oil for frying

DIRECTIONS

1. Sift the flour, baking powder, salt, baking soda, and nutmeg together in a medium bowl. Set aside. Whisk the buttermilk, eggs, and vanilla together in a small bowl.

2. Place the butter and 1 cup of the sugar in the bowl of a stand mixer fitted with the paddle attachment. Beat on medium speed until light and fluffy, 1 to 2 minutes.

3. Beginning and ending with the dry ingredients, alternately add the dry ingredients and buttermilk to the mixer, beating after each addition to combine. Beat until the dough is soft and completely combined, about 1 minute. It will be sticky.

4. Remove the bowl from the mixer and tightly cover with plastic wrap. Refrigerate for at least 1 hour or overnight.

5. Line a rimmed baking sheet with parchment paper. Pour the remaining 1 cup sugar onto a plate or shallow bowl.

6. Fill a Dutch oven or large heavy pot 2 inches deep with vegetable oil. Heat to 325°F. When the oil is heated, use an ice cream scoop or large spoon to scoop 2- to 3-tablespoon-size balls and drop directly into the oil. Cook three or four doughnuts at a time until golden brown and crispy, 3 to 4 minutes per side. Repeat with the remaining dough.

7. While still warm, coat the doughnuts in sugar and place on a wire rack or serving plate. Serve immediately.

Note

These are best enjoyed immediately after frying (and won't last more than a few hours), but you can refrigerate the dough for up to three days and fry on-demand for super fresh, crispy doughnuts.

Wild Rice Pancakes

Makes about eight 6-inch pancakes

I originally set out to create a riff on classic diner pancakes, but it's hard to improve on an icon! Instead, this recipe takes the basic buttermilk batter and adds texture and flavor with wild rice (also a great source of fiber and protein). I love these slightly savory pancakes combined with a sweet and tangy berry compote, but you can serve them with butter and maple syrup if you prefer.

LINGONBERRY & BLUEBERRY COMPOTE

1 pint blueberries

½ cup lingonberry preserves

¼ cup sugar

2 tablespoons water

2 teaspoons lemon zest

WILD RICE PANCAKES

2 cups all-purpose flour

2 tablespoons sugar

2 teaspoons baking powder

1 teaspoon baking soda

¾ teaspoon kosher salt

1½ cups milk or buttermilk

2 eggs

3 tablespoons melted butter, plus more for griddle

1 cup cooked wild rice (from about ¼ cup uncooked rice; see Note on page 65)

DIRECTIONS

1. **MAKE THE COMPOTE:** Place 1 cup of the blueberries, lingonberry preserves, sugar, water, and lemon zest in a small saucepan. Bring to a simmer over medium-low heat and cook for 3 to 5 minutes, until thick and jammy. Stir in the remaining blueberries and let sit at room temperature. Compote can be made up to 1 week ahead.

2. **MAKE THE PANCAKES:** Whisk the flour, sugar, baking powder, baking soda, and salt together in a large bowl. Make a well in the center and add the milk, eggs, and melted butter to the well. Gradually whisk the wet ingredients into the dry ingredients until just combined (a few dry spots are okay). Stir in the wild rice.

3. Heat a griddle over medium-low for 5 minutes. Coat with butter. Use a ½ cup measuring cup to ladle pancake batter onto the griddle, cooking two pancakes at a time. Cook the pancakes for about 2 minutes, until the bottom is golden brown. Flip and cook for 2 minutes on the other side. Repeat with the remaining batter.

4. Serve the pancakes with the berry compote.

APPETIZERS

Cocktail parties are the best parties.

There's something about the sound: close your eyes and you can hear clinking glasses, laughter, the hum of conversation, the tinkle of ice hitting a cocktail shaker. You hear those sounds, and you know it's going to be a good night.

As an inveterate grazer, the other thing I love about cocktail parties is the food—instead of having to choose one entrée, you get to sample all kinds of salty snacks (the best kind!). Who doesn't want a dinner made up of deviled eggs, fried potato balls, olives, and cheese? I'd choose that over a roast chicken or steak nine times out of ten.

The recipes in this chapter are well suited to a cocktail party, with a variety of flavors and textures, but they're also great as the prelude to a sit-down dinner, or as lunch on their own. Apple Gjetost Grilled Cheese (page 31) is a tasty introduction to the pleasures of caramel-like Norwegian brown cheese, while the Sour Cream, Shallot & Ramp Dip (page 44) elevates the classic dip with fresh ingredients but is still ready in under half an hour. A variety of fried, salty treats never go amiss, and tender Beer-Battered Shrimp with Herb Sour Cream (page 32) or savory Norwegian Potato Balls (page 40) are a welcome addition to happy hour at our house. (Of course, all are especially good when accompanied by something cold—up to you if that's a bracing shot of aquavit.)

A cocktail party is also something you can throw together with little effort for last-minute gatherings. Instead of a multicourse meal, an array of dips, pickles, fried shrimp, and open-faced sandwiches, plus a couple of trays of Aquavit Martinis (page 160) or Lingonberry Old-Fashioneds (page 186) feels casual yet festive, no matter the time of year. No need for fancy place settings, or matching glasses and flatware. Simply turn on some music, chill the drinks, and enjoy the party.

Apple Gjetost Grilled Cheese   31

Beer-Battered Shrimp with Herb Sour Cream   32

Deviled Eggs   35

Hot Salmon Dip   36

Whipped Salt Cod Spread   37

Lefse Pinwheels   39

Norwegian Potato Balls   40

Shrimp Salad on Toast   43

Sour Cream, Shallot & Ramp Dip   44

Tomato Toast with Homemade Mayonnaise   46

Apple Gjetost Grilled Cheese

Serves 4 to 8

Gjetost is a sweet, caramel-like cheese derived from the leftover whey from making goat cheese, and it is very popular in Norway. It's often used in a sweeter application, such as a dessert fondue, or it's served with jam on toast for breakfast. I like to harness its creamy texture and caramelized flavor in more savory applications, such as this grilled cheese. When paired with sharp cheddar and a homemade apple mostarda, it's an unreal combination.

You'll have leftover mostarda, but save the extra for butter-basted Pork Chops with Apple Mostarda (page 149) or spread it on toast with cream cheese or melted Brie. For a simplified version of this recipe, skip the mostarda and instead layer each sandwich with some whole-grain Dijon mustard and a few sautéed apple slices.

APPLE MOSTARDA

2 pounds apples (about 4 large), such as Honeycrisp or Gala, peeled, cored, and diced

½ cup packed brown sugar

2 tablespoons mustard seeds

1 tablespoon chopped fresh thyme leaves

2 teaspoons lemon zest

1 teaspoon kosher salt

½ teaspoon ground pepper

½ cup apple cider vinegar

½ cup apple juice, cider, or water

GRILLED CHEESE

8 slices country style or sourdough bread

2 to 4 tablespoons butter, softened

2 ounces sharp cheddar cheese, sliced ¼ inch thick

2 ounces gjetost, sliced ¼ inch thick

DIRECTIONS

1. **MAKE THE APPLE MOSTARDA:** Combine the apples, brown sugar, mustard seeds, thyme, lemon zest, salt, and pepper in a large saucepan or Dutch oven. Bring to a boil over medium-high heat, then reduce the heat to a simmer and cover. Stir in the vinegar and apple juice. Cook, stirring occasionally, until the mostarda becomes thick and jammy, 1½ to 2 hours. Cover and refrigerate for up to one month.

2. **MAKE THE APPLE GJETOST GRILLED CHEESE:** Preheat a large skillet or griddle over medium-low heat. Spread each slice of bread with butter on one side. Divide the cheddar and gjetost between four slices of bread and spread each with about ¼ cup mostarda. Top with the remaining bread slices.

3. Cook the sandwiches two at a time until the bread is toasted and the cheese is melted, flipping once, 5 to 8 minutes total. Repeat with remaining sandwiches. Cut into squares or triangles and serve warm.

Beer-Battered Shrimp with Herb Sour Cream

Serves 4 to 6

Deep-frying can feel intimidating, but once you get the hang of it, it's a cinch. The key items? An instant-read thermometer to check the oil temperature and a large pot with high sides—I use my Dutch oven, but my parents use their electric wok. For these crispy fried shrimp, I dredge them in a simple beer batter and serve with tangy sour cream spiked with fresh herbs. If you're not a beer drinker, or don't have any on hand, seltzer works well.

HERB SOUR CREAM

¾ cup sour cream or Greek yogurt

¼ cup mayonnaise

2 tablespoons chopped fresh herbs, such as dill, parsley, chives, or basil

1 tablespoon chopped capers

1 tablespoon lemon juice

Kosher salt

Ground pepper

BEER-BATTERED SHRIMP

2 pounds peeled and deveined shrimp

1 teaspoon kosher salt, plus more for seasoning

Ground pepper

1½ cups all-purpose flour

1½ teaspoons baking powder

1 teaspoon garlic powder

½ teaspoon cayenne

Canola or vegetable oil for frying

1½ cups lager

Lemon wedges for serving

DIRECTIONS

1. **MAKE THE HERB SOUR CREAM:** Mix the sour cream, mayonnaise, herbs, capers, and lemon juice in a small bowl. Season to taste with salt and pepper. Refrigerate until ready to use.

2. **MAKE THE BEER-BATTERED SHRIMP:** Pat the shrimp dry and season with salt and pepper. Whisk the flour, baking powder, 1 teaspoon salt, garlic powder, and cayenne together in a large bowl.

3. Fill a deep saucepan or Dutch oven 2 inches deep with the oil. Set over medium heat until the oil reaches 375°F.

4. Just before the oil reaches the temperature, add the beer to the flour mixture. Whisk until just combined (it will be lumpy). Working in batches, add the shrimp to the batter and flip to coat.

5. Working quickly, add a few battered shrimp to the oil and fry until golden brown, about 3 minutes. Use a slotted spoon to transfer to a paper towel–lined plate or wire rack and season with salt. Repeat with the remaining shrimp.

6. Serve the shrimp immediately with the Herb Sour Cream and lemon wedges.

Deviled Eggs

Makes 12

In my experience, deviled eggs are always one of the first appetizers to disappear at any gathering—but in case you end up with leftovers, just chop them up and mix with a little more mayo for egg salad. I love to top these with a variety of pickled and salty things, but you can keep it classic with minced chives and smoked paprika if you prefer.

6 large eggs

¼ cup mayonnaise

1 tablespoon sour cream

1 tablespoon chopped chives,
  plus more for garnish

1 teaspoon whole-grain mustard

1 teaspoon lemon juice

½ teaspoon kosher salt

¼ teaspoon ground pepper

GARNISH CHOICES

Chives

Quick Pickled Shallots (page 39)
  or Mixed Pickled Vegetables (page 112)

Smoked salmon

Salmon or trout roe

Crumbled bacon

Smoked paprika

DIRECTIONS

1. Place the eggs in a large saucepan and cover with water 1 inch above the eggs. Cover the pan and bring the water to a boil, then remove the pan from the heat and let sit for 9 minutes. Transfer the eggs from the pan into a bowl filled with cold water. Crack the eggs and peel to remove shell (this works best with older eggs, but if you have fresh eggs, crack them and then return to cold water before peeling to make it easier to remove the shell).

2. Cut each egg in half lengthwise and scoop out the yolks into a medium bowl. Cover and refrigerate the egg whites if making ahead.

3. Add the mayonnaise, sour cream, 1 tablespoon chives, mustard, lemon juice, salt, and pepper to the bowl with the egg yolks. Mash with a fork until well combined.

4. Transfer the egg yolk mixture into a piping bag fitted with your choice of tip or a sealable plastic bag with a ¼-inch hole cut in one corner. Pipe the filling into the egg white halves.

5. Top the eggs with your choice of garnish, such as chives, Quick Pickled Shallots or Mixed Pickled Vegetables, smoked salmon, roe, crumbled bacon, and/or smoked paprika. Serve immediately, or cover and refrigerate for up to 6 hours.

Hot Salmon Dip

Serves 6

I would happily eat smoked salmon with cream cheese any time of day, but this easy dip is particularly perfect for cocktail hour, best served with an ice-cold martini or glass of white wine. In the unlikely scenario you end up with any left over, I highly recommend spreading it on a toasted bagel with your morning coffee. It's also delicious with Norwegian Rye Bread (page 88), toasted baguette slices, rye crackers, sliced cucumbers, radishes, carrots, or pita chips.

8 ounces cream cheese, room temperature

½ cup sour cream

½ cup grated mozzarella cheese

½ cup minced shallots

1 tablespoon lemon juice

½ teaspoon kosher salt

¼ teaspoon ground pepper

4 ounces hot-smoked salmon, flaked

¼ cup grated Parmesan cheese

1 tablespoon chopped fresh chives

Salmon or trout roe (optional)

DIRECTIONS

1. Preheat oven to 375°F. Coat a 2-cup baking dish or ramekin with baking spray.

2. Place the cream cheese, sour cream, mozzarella, shallots, lemon juice, salt, and pepper in the bowl of a stand mixer fitted with the paddle attachment. Mix on medium speed until very smooth, about 1 minute. Alternatively, mix vigorously in a bowl with a wooden spoon until smooth. Remove from the mixer and stir in the salmon.

3. Spread the salmon mixture in the prepared baking dish. Sprinkle with the Parmesan cheese. Bake until the dip is golden brown and begins to bubble, about 20 minutes. If desired, broil for 1 to 2 minutes to brown the top.

4. Sprinkle with the chives and serve with salmon roe if desired.

Whipped Salt Cod Spread

Makes about 3 cups

Inspired by the French dish brandade, this creamy dip features salt cod, one of Norway's oldest and most widely available exports. Be sure to start this recipe at least one day before you plan to serve it, as the salt cod needs to soak for 24 hours before cooking.

1 pound salt cod filets (see Note)

4 ounces Yukon Gold potatoes (about 2 large), peeled and cut into 1-inch pieces

Kosher salt

2 cups milk

4 garlic cloves

2 bay leaves, preferably fresh

¼ cup olive oil, plus more for drizzling

½ cup heavy whipping cream

Ground pepper

Zest of 1 lemon

¼ cup chopped fresh parsley or chives

Toasted baguette slices or Flatbrød (page 89) for serving

Crudités for serving

DIRECTIONS

1. **AT LEAST 1 DAY AHEAD:** Rinse the salt from the surface of the cod. Place the cod in a large bowl filled with cold water. Refrigerate for 24 hours, changing the water several times throughout soaking.

2. Meanwhile, place the potatoes in a large saucepan. Cover with water and season generously with salt. Bring to a boil and cook until very tender, about 15 minutes. Drain and use a ricer or masher to mash the potatoes. Refrigerate until ready to use.

3. When ready to cook, drain the cod and place in a medium saucepan. Cover with the milk and add the garlic and bay leaves. Bring to a simmer and cook until the fish is tender and beginning to flake apart, 25 to 30 minutes. Drain the fish and the garlic into a colander. Discard the bay leaves.

4. Break the fish into pieces and transfer the fish and garlic cloves to the bowl of a food processor, discarding the bones and any skin. Add reserved potatoes. With the processor running, slowly add the olive oil, then the whipping cream, until the mixture is very smooth and creamy. Season with salt and pepper and stir in the lemon zest.

5. Transfer the salt cod spread to a serving bowl. Drizzle with olive oil and top with parsley. Serve with baguette slices, flatbrød, or crudités. If not serving immediately, cover and refrigerate for up to 5 days, or freeze for up to 3 months.

Note

You can find salt cod at seafood markets, in the freezer or seafood section of well-stocked grocery stores, and online.

Lefse Pinwheels

Makes 35 to 40

Lefse is a Norwegian potato flatbread that's notoriously finicky to make but remains a staple in Norwegian American households across the Midwest. I grew up eating it with butter and sugar, but these days I prefer it in a more savory application—in this case, rolled with cream cheese, cured salmon, capers, and cucumbers à la bagels and lox. In Scandinavia, lefse is often used as a sandwich wrap for sausages, cheese, and more. You can make it at home (Lefse, page 86), find it online, or simply use flour tortillas instead.

QUICK PICKLED SHALLOTS

½ cup white vinegar

¼ cup water

1 teaspoon kosher salt

1 teaspoon sugar

1 large shallot, thinly sliced

LEFSE PINWHEELS

4 ounces cream cheese, room temperature

½ cup sour cream, room temperature

½ cup capers, drained

6 Lefse (page 86) or 10-inch flour tortillas

1 small English cucumber, sliced paper thin lengthwise with a mandolin or very sharp knife

8 ounces lox or homemade Gravlax (page 172)

DIRECTIONS

1. **MAKE THE QUICK PICKLED SHALLOTS:** Heat the vinegar, water, salt, and sugar in a small saucepan over medium heat. Bring to a simmer and stir until the salt and sugar have dissolved.

2. Pour the vinegar mixture over the sliced shallots in a small bowl. Let sit at room temperature for 30 minutes.

3. **MAKE THE LEFSE PINWHEELS:** In the bowl of a stand mixer or food processor, beat the cream cheese and sour cream until well combined. Remove from the mixer and stir in the capers.

4. Spread the lefse with the cream cheese mixture in an even layer. Layer the cucumber slices and lox over the cream cheese. Scatter the pickled shallots over the lox. Tightly roll each lefse into a log and wrap tightly in plastic wrap.

5. Refrigerate for 1 hour. When ready to serve, cut each log into 1½-inch pieces.

Norwegian Potato Balls

Makes about 40

The anchovies in these crispy fried treats are optional, but highly encouraged! They add delicious umami flavor, but if you're not a fan, you could also stir in ½ cup grated Parmesan cheese instead. This tasty appetizer is also a great way to use up leftover mashed potatoes—just add anchovies, flour, and parsley, and adjust the seasoning as needed.

1 pound Yukon Gold potatoes, peeled and cut into 1-inch pieces

¼ cup whole milk

2 tablespoons butter

8 anchovies, finely chopped (optional)

¼ cup chopped parsley, plus more for garnish

2 garlic cloves, minced

1 tablespoon all-purpose flour, plus more if needed

½ teaspoon kosher salt

½ teaspoon ground mustard

¼ teaspoon ground pepper

Pinch of nutmeg

2 eggs

2 cups panko bread crumbs

Vegetable or canola oil for frying

Flaky sea salt, such as Maldon

Lemon wedges for serving

Homemade Mayonnaise (page 46) for serving

DIRECTIONS

1. Place the potatoes in a medium saucepan. Fill with water. Bring to a boil over high heat, then reduce heat to medium and cook until potatoes are tender, about 15 minutes. Drain and return the potatoes to the pan.

2. Add the milk and butter to the potatoes and mash until no lumps remain. Let sit at room temperature until cool enough to touch. You'll have about 2 cups of mashed potatoes.

3. Add the anchovies, chopped parsley, garlic, flour, salt, mustard, pepper, and nutmeg to the potatoes. Mix well. The mixture should be fairly firm and hold its shape when formed into balls. Add more flour if needed. Use an ice cream scoop or spoon to shape into 1-tablespoon-size balls and place on a rimmed baking sheet. They will be sticky—wetting your hands every so often can help with this.

4. Place the eggs in a shallow bowl and whisk together. Place the panko bread crumbs on a small plate. Dip the potato balls into the egg, then into the bread crumbs, coating completely. Return them to the baking sheet. Refrigerate the potato balls for at least 30 minutes, or up to 1 day.

5. Add 2 inches of vegetable oil to a deep saucepan or Dutch oven. Heat to 350°F.

6. Fry the potato balls a few at a time until golden brown and crispy, flipping as needed, 2 to 3 minutes total. Drain on a paper towel–lined plate.

7. Sprinkle the potato balls with chopped parsley and flaky sea salt. Serve with lemon wedges and Homemade Mayonnaise.

Note

These potato balls can be made up to three days ahead and reheated. To serve, spread the cooked potato balls on a rimmed baking sheet and heat in a 350°F oven for 5 to 10 minutes.

Shrimp Salad on Toast

Serves 8 as an appetizer, or 4 as a light main course

This is my take on one of the classic smørrebrød, aka Danish open-faced sandwiches. Buy the smallest shrimp you can. If you can find only jumbo shrimp, simply chop them into pieces before mixing. This salad would also be delicious with other types of seafood, such as crab or lobster, for a light spring or summer lunch.

1 pound raw small to large shrimp, peeled and deveined

2 tablespoons Homemade Mayonnaise (page 46) or store-bought

2 tablespoons sour cream

2 tablespoons lemon juice, plus more if desired

½ teaspoon horseradish

¼ teaspoon kosher salt

3 tablespoons softened salted butter

8 slices rye bread or country-style bread, toasted

2 avocados, pitted and thinly sliced

Flaky sea salt for garnish

1 cup watercress or arugula

Chopped dill for garnish

DIRECTIONS

1. Bring a large pot of salted water to boil. Add the shrimp and poach until pink and opaque, 2 to 3 minutes. Drain and refrigerate until cool.

2. Place the mayonnaise, sour cream, 1 tablespoon of the lemon juice, horseradish, and salt in a large bowl. Stir to combine. Add the cooled shrimp and stir to coat.

3. Spread the butter evenly onto each slice of rye bread. Place a few avocado slices onto each piece of bread. Season with the flaky sea salt and remaining 1 tablespoon lemon juice.

4. Divide the watercress between the bread slices. Top with the shrimp salad and sprinkle with dill. Squeeze more lemon over the toasts if desired. Serve immediately.

Sour Cream, Shallot & Ramp Dip

Makes about 1½ cups

This recipe is inspired by the classic (and extremely easy-to-make and delicious) Lipton sour cream dip, as well as a wonderful version by recipe developer Genevieve Ko from the *Los Angeles Times*. In her recipe, Genevieve browns chopped onions with salt, then simply combines them with sour cream for a slightly healthier, three-ingredient take on the original.

I love the pungent flavor of shallots, and when blended with spring ramps and rich sour cream, the combination is irresistible. While I often make this dip in late spring to take advantage of ramps' short season, you can also use garlic scapes or green onions year-round with great results. Make this a couple of hours before serving to let the alliums and dairy meld, or preferably the day before for maximum flavor. Serve with potato chips, pita chips, or your choice of vegetables.

2 tablespoons olive oil

½ cup chopped shallots

½ cup chopped ramps (bulbs, stems, and leaves), plus more for garnish

½ teaspoon kosher salt, plus more if needed

1 cup sour cream

DIRECTIONS

1. Heat the olive oil in a small saucepan over medium-low. Add the shallots and ramps, and cook until tender and browned, about 15 minutes. Season with salt.

2. Use a slotted spoon to transfer the shallots and ramps to a medium bowl. Reserve the cooking oil. Add the sour cream and stir to combine. Season with more salt if needed.

3. Cover and refrigerate for at least 1 hour and preferably overnight. Drizzle with the reserved cooking oil and garnish with additional chopped ramps before serving.

Tomato Toast with Homemade Mayonnaise

Serves 4

My mom's tomato harvest every year is epic, and my parents make tomato-basil bruschetta at least once a week in the summertime. This is my favorite way to eat peak-season heirloom tomatoes, with a nod to the mayo-heavy salads and dips common in the Midwest. Making homemade mayo is a breeze once you get the hang of it—the key is starting with room-temperature egg yolks and adding a little acid for stability—but this dish would still be delicious with Hellmann's or your favorite store-bought mayo. Grilling the bread adds a complex smoky, charred flavor, but you can also toast it in a 400°F oven until golden brown.

HOMEMADE MAYONNAISE

2 garlic cloves

Up to 1 teaspoon kosher salt

1 egg yolk, at room temperature (see Note)

Juice of ½ lemon, plus more as needed

½ cup olive oil

½ cup canola oil

TOMATO TOAST

4 slices rustic bread, such as sourdough or pain au levain

⅓ cup olive oil

2 to 4 heirloom tomatoes, depending on size

Flaky sea salt, such as Maldon

1 tablespoon fresh oregano leaves

DIRECTIONS

1. **MAKE THE HOMEMADE MAYONNAISE:** Mince the garlic, adding a pinch of salt as you chop until it forms a rough paste. Place the garlic in a medium bowl and whisk in the egg yolk. Whisk in a few drops of the lemon juice (this helps keep the mayo stable).

2. Combine the olive and canola oils in a measuring cup with a spout or small pitcher. Add the oil in a very slow stream to the egg, whisking constantly or using a hand blender. Alternatively, place the egg and garlic in a food processor or blender and add the oils in a slow stream while blending.

3. The mixture will be very creamy and thick. Add the remaining lemon juice and salt to taste. Refrigerate for up to 2 weeks.

4. **MAKE THE TOMATO TOAST:** Preheat a grill or cast-iron grill pan over medium-high heat and brush with oil. Generously brush each slice of bread with olive oil on both sides. Grill until browned and grill marks are visible, 2 to 3 minutes per side.

5. **ASSEMBLE TOAST:** Slice each tomato crosswise. Slather mayo onto each slice of bread, then top with tomato slices. Sprinkle with flaky sea salt and oregano leaves. Serve immediately.

SOUPS
& SALADS

I grew up with vivid and differentiated seasons, but it took moving to California to really appreciate them.

Getting used to 70 degrees and sunshine nearly year-round didn't take long. But when Ari and I moved back to Minnesota in 2020, after spending five years in a pleasant climate, I was surprised at how much I loved experiencing all four seasons. We arrived in September, just in time for the last gasp of warm summer weather (and late-season tomatoes), then marveled at the crisp evenings and beautiful fall colors as October gave way to November.

Winter in Minnesota is rarely celebrated outside of the state, with many questioning why one would want to live in a place known for the harshest winters in the country. And the winter weather can be brutal, with temperatures regularly dipping below zero and snowstorms that can occur well into April. But I also forgot how much I love the winter—the stillness, the stark beauty of bare trees in the snow, the cozy feeling of coming inside to a warm fire after a brisk walk in the cold. Perhaps we will get tired of shoveling snow and waiting for the car to warm up, but for now, we revel in it with a warm bowl of Chicken Wild Rice Soup (the ultimate comfort food, page 68) and wait for spring.

Springtime comes slowly here, the cold weather seeming to drag on well past its expiration date. But as surely as the crocuses poke their buds through the cold ground in March, early spring produce like ramps and rhubarb arrives and we remember what it's like to subsist on more than potatoes and winter squash. In springtime, a simple Butter Lettuce Salad with Creamy Mustard Dressing (page 52) makes the most of these delicate vegetables, as a light first course or accompaniment to roast chicken or fish.

And finally, summer. Summer in the Midwest is kind of magical, the daily humidity building into volatile thunderstorms, giving way to sunny days. The heat can be miserable, but that heat also makes ice cream extra refreshing, lake swims feel more invigorating, and fresh tomatoes taste that much sweeter. California's produce may be of superior quality throughout the entire year, but one Midwest staple can't be beat during the height of summer: sweet corn. When eaten raw it's practically candy, when kissed by the searing heat of the grill and seasoned with salt and a slather of butter, it's heaven. You can find it sold on the side of the road across the region in late summer, and if you're lucky enough to come across it, I promise it'll be some of the best few dollars you'll ever spend. Dressing it up in Corn Salad with Dill & Goat Cheese (page 55) or Smoked Trout Corn Chowder (page 71) this time of year isn't strictly necessary, but I usually find myself with an overabundance of corn and always look for new ways to use it. And then before we know it, the warm days of August give way to cool fall nights, and the colors change again.

Butter Lettuce Salad with Creamy
Mustard Dressing   52

Corn Salad with Dill & Goat Cheese   55

Cabbage Salad with Caraway Seeds   56

Tomato Salad with Crispy Rye
Bread Crumbs   59

Grilled Wedge Salad   60

Buttermilk Herb Dressing   62

Apple & Fennel Salad   63

Wild Rice Salad with Butternut Squash &
Pomegranates   64

Butternut Squash & Apple Soup   67

Chicken Wild Rice Soup   68

Smoked Trout Corn Chowder   71

Butter Lettuce Salad with Creamy Mustard Dressing

Serves 4 to 6

I'm a big fan of butter lettuce in all forms, and when creating this recipe I wanted to make something that highlighted the flavor and texture of peak spring lettuce. This fits the bill: The creamy mustard dressing (thanks to the egg yolk) is a perfect foil for the delicate greens and crisp sliced radishes. For a heartier meal, stir in some cold shredded chicken or salmon.

CREAMY MUSTARD DRESSING

2 tablespoons Dijon mustard

1 tablespoon white vinegar or lemon juice

1 egg yolk, room temperature

½ cup olive oil

2 tablespoons minced shallots

½ teaspoon honey

½ teaspoon kosher salt

¼ teaspoon ground pepper

BUTTER LETTUCE SALAD

1 head butter or Bibb lettuce, washed and torn into 1-inch pieces

4 radishes, trimmed and very thinly sliced

Kosher salt

Ground pepper

½ cup shaved Parmesan cheese (optional)

DIRECTIONS

1. **MAKE THE CREAMY MUSTARD DRESSING:** Place the mustard, vinegar, and egg yolk in a medium bowl and whisk to combine. Add the olive oil in a slow, steady stream, whisking constantly, until the dressing is emulsified and very creamy. Whisk in the shallots, honey, salt, and pepper. If making ahead, refrigerate until ready to use.

2. Place the lettuce and radishes in a large serving bowl. Season with salt and pepper. Add ½ cup of the dressing and toss well to coat. Add more dressing as desired. Sprinkle with Parmesan shavings if you like.

Corn Salad with Dill & Goat Cheese

Serves 4 to 6

Loosely inspired by Mexican elote, it's hard to beat the combination of corn, salty cheese, and fresh herbs in this refreshing side dish. I make this all summer long with different flavors—instead of dill and goat cheese, try cilantro and cotija, parsley and feta, or oregano and ricotta salata. The options are endless!

QUICK PICKLED RED ONIONS

¼ cup unseasoned rice vinegar

1 teaspoon sugar

¼ teaspoon kosher salt

½ small red onion, peeled and thinly sliced

CORN SALAD

8 ears corn

¼ cup olive oil

1 tablespoon lemon juice

1 teaspoon kosher salt, plus more if needed

½ teaspoon ground pepper, plus more if needed

1 cup crumbled goat cheese (4 ounces)

½ cup chopped dill

DIRECTIONS

1. **MAKE THE PICKLED RED ONIONS:** Whisk the vinegar, sugar, and salt together in a small bowl. Add the onions and let sit for 30 minutes, or refrigerate for up to 3 days.

2. **MAKE THE CORN SALAD:** Preheat a grill to medium heat. Shuck the corn. Grill until the kernels begin to pop and the corn is slightly charred on all sides, about 15 minutes. Alternatively, place the corn directly over a gas flame and turn them with tongs to char on all sides. Let them cool for a few minutes, then cut the kernels from the cob with a serrated knife. Place in a large bowl.

3. Whisk the olive oil, lemon juice, salt, and pepper together in a small bowl. Strain the onions and whisk in the pickling liquid. Whisk in the goat cheese until smooth. (You can also make this in a blender or with an immersion blender.)

4. Add the red onions and dill to the bowl with the corn. Mix well. Drizzle with the goat cheese dressing and stir gently to coat. Season with additional salt and pepper if needed. Serve immediately.

Cabbage Salad with Caraway Seeds

Serves 8 to 10

The original recipe that inspired this one included a packet of gelatin in the dressing, so I'm guessing it was meant to be a molded salad served as part of a buffet. I prefer my cabbage slaw on the crunchy side, so instead of a molded salad I used some of the original spices, added caraway, and swapped the gelatin for a tangy vinaigrette. Caraway is commonly used when making sauerkraut, and it works well with cabbage. This fresh slaw is always welcome on my table as part of a spread with glazed ham, to add texture to fried fish sandwiches, or as a side dish at summer barbecues.

DRESSING

2 teaspoons caraway seeds
¼ cup white vinegar
¼ cup lemon juice
2 tablespoons mayonnaise
1 tablespoon sugar
1 teaspoon kosher salt
1 teaspoon ground pepper
½ cup olive oil

CABBAGE SALAD

1 head green cabbage, cored and shredded
1 fennel bulb, trimmed, white and light green parts thinly sliced, fronds reserved
1 red onion, thinly sliced
½ cup fresh dill or parsley, roughly chopped, for garnish

DIRECTIONS

1. **MAKE THE DRESSING:** Heat a small skillet over medium heat. Add the caraway seeds and toast them until fragrant, stirring constantly, 2 to 3 minutes. Transfer the seeds to a spice grinder or mortar and pestle. Crush until roughly ground.

2. Add the caraway seeds, vinegar, lemon juice, mayonnaise, sugar, salt, and pepper to a large serving bowl. Whisk until combined. Slowly drizzle in the olive oil, whisking constantly, until the dressing is emulsified.

3. **MAKE THE SALAD:** Add the cabbage, fennel, and red onion to the bowl with the dressing. Use your hands or tongs to toss until the salad is well coated. Garnish with fresh herbs and fennel fronds. Let sit for 15 minutes before serving, or cover and refrigerate for up to 4 hours.

Tomato Salad with Crispy Rye Bread Crumbs

Serves 4 to 6

Peak-season tomatoes don't need much more than a sprinkle of salt to be thoroughly enjoyed, but on those occasions when you want to dress them up a little more, this salad is a great way to do it. While I love a good panzanella or caprese salad, the earthy rye bread crumbs, tangy goat cheese dressing, and fresh herbs in this recipe combine for a unique spin on the iconic Italian dish.

CRISPY RYE BREAD CRUMBS

4 slices rye bread, homemade if desired (Norwegian Rye Bread, page 88)

3 tablespoons olive oil

½ teaspoon kosher salt

TOMATO SALAD

4 ounces goat cheese, room temperature

½ cup buttermilk

½ teaspoon ground pepper

2 pounds mixed heirloom tomatoes, cut into ½-inch-thick slices

Flaky sea salt, such as Maldon

½ cup chopped fresh herbs, such as basil, tarragon, marjoram, or chives

DIRECTIONS

1. **MAKE THE BREAD CRUMBS:** Place the rye bread in the body of a food processor. Process until large crumbs form, about 30 seconds. You should have about 1¼ cups of bread crumbs.

2. Heat the olive oil in a skillet over medium heat. Add the bread crumbs and stir to coat. Cook until fragrant, golden brown, and crispy, stirring frequently, 5 to 8 minutes. Sprinkle with kosher salt and set aside.

3. **MAKE THE SALAD:** Place the goat cheese and buttermilk in a small bowl. Whisk until smooth. Season with the ground pepper.

4. Layer the tomatoes on a serving platter or bowl. Sprinkle with the flaky sea salt. Drizzle with the goat cheese dressing, then sprinkle with the bread crumbs and chopped herbs.

Note

You'll have extra bread crumbs. Use them on the Grilled Wedge Salad (page 60) or Gjetost Mac & Cheese (page 81), or save them in a sealed container for up to 1 month. You can also freeze them for up to 6 months.

Grilled Wedge Salad

Serves 4

In ideal summer fashion, all the components of this salad can be prepared on the grill (including the bread crumbs, if you use an ovenproof skillet!). If you like, you can leave the iceberg lettuce raw, but grilling it adds an amazing smoky, charred flavor that creates a wonderful contrast to the creamy dressing. This salad makes for a rich side with Juicy Lucy's (page 146), Fried Walleye Sandwiches (page 132), or Cornflake-Crusted Chicken (page 128), but I like to serve it as a retro starter for summer dinner parties. It easily can be doubled to feed larger parties—just be sure you have enough dressing.

8 bacon slices

2 ears corn, shucked

4 green onions or 1 bunch chives

1 head iceberg lettuce, cut into quarters lengthwise

½ cup olive oil

Kosher salt

Ground pepper

TO SERVE

1 cup Buttermilk Herb Dressing (page 62)

1 cup Crispy Rye Bread Crumbs (page 59)

1 cup cherry tomatoes, cut in half

DIRECTIONS

1. Preheat a grill to medium heat. Line a rimmed baking sheet with foil and place a wire rack on top. Lay the bacon on the rack and place on the grill. Cover and cook for 12 to 15 minutes, until crisp and golden brown. Set aside to cool. Alternatively, cook in the same way in an oven at 400°F. If you have a smaller charcoal grill, lay the bacon in a single layer in a cast-iron skillet. Cover and cook over medium heat for 12 to 15 minutes, until crisp and golden brown. Drain on paper towels.

2. Brush the corn, green onions, and lettuce quarters with the olive oil and season with salt and pepper. Place on a rimmed baking sheet.

3. Beginning with the corn and green onions, grill over medium-high heat until charred and tender, about 10 minutes. Repeat with the lettuce, about 3 minutes per side. Return all the vegetables to the baking sheet.

4. **TO ASSEMBLE:** Crumble the bacon into small pieces. Use a serrated knife to cut the kernels from the corncobs. Roughly chop the green onions and discard the roots. Place each quarter of the lettuce on a serving plate. Sprinkle each plate with the corn and green onions. Drizzle the lettuce with the dressing, then sprinkle with bread crumbs, crumbled bacon, and cherry tomatoes. Serve immediately.

Buttermilk Herb Dressing

Makes about 2 cups

This dressing is basically a homemade take on ranch dressing, the condiment that made me learn to like vegetables and one that I love to this day. The creamy, zippy dressing pairs perfectly with crunchy green vegetables. I use it on Green Beans & Snap Peas with Buttermilk Herb Dressing (page 101) and Grilled Wedge Salad (page 60), but it also makes a delicious dip for crudités or tater tots. You might want to go ahead and make a double batch.

¼ cup fresh dill

¼ cup fresh chives

3 tablespoons fresh parsley

1 small shallot, minced

1 garlic clove, minced

¾ cup buttermilk

½ cup sour cream or Greek yogurt

¼ cup mayonnaise

¼ cup lemon juice, plus more if needed

1 teaspoon Worcestershire sauce

Kosher salt

Ground pepper

DIRECTIONS

1. Place the dill, chives, and parsley on a cutting board. Finely chop. Transfer to a small bowl with the minced shallots and garlic and stir to combine.

2. Whisk in the buttermilk, sour cream, mayonnaise, lemon juice, and Worcestershire sauce until well blended. Season with salt and pepper. Taste and add more lemon juice, salt, or pepper as needed.

3. Store the dressing in the refrigerator for up to 1 week.

Note

If you're not a fan of dill, substitute more fresh parsley or tarragon.

Apple & Fennel Salad

Serves 4 to 6

Apple and fennel are naturally complementary, and the bright crunch of this salad makes for a lively fall and winter side dish when tossed with a simple honey-shallot vinaigrette. I'm not a big fan of celery, but if you are, a thinly sliced stalk or two would be an excellent addition. Serve with roast chicken or pork chops, or as a light Thanksgiving or holiday side dish.

Juice of 1 lemon (about ¼ cup)

2 tablespoons minced shallots

1 tablespoon honey

¼ cup olive oil

4 cups arugula or watercress

2 apples, cored and thinly sliced

1 fennel bulb, trimmed, cored, and very thinly sliced

Kosher salt

Ground pepper

2 ounces crumbled goat cheese

½ cup toasted almonds or hazelnuts, roughly chopped

¼ cup chopped fresh fennel fronds, parsley, or dill

DIRECTIONS

1. Add the lemon juice, shallots, and honey to a large serving bowl. Whisk to combine. Whisk in the olive oil in a slow stream.

2. Add the arugula, apples, and fennel to the bowl with the dressing. Season well with salt and pepper. Use tongs or your hands to coat the vegetables with the dressing.

3. Sprinkle the salad with the goat cheese, nuts, and fresh herbs. Serve immediately.

Wild Rice Salad with Butternut Squash & Pomegranates

Serves 4 to 6

Filled with different textures and flavors, this fall side highlights one of Minnesota's best known native plants, wild rice, and combines it with sweet roasted squash, creamy goat cheese, and zippy pomegranate seeds. This salad is a tasty side dish for Thanksgiving dinner or other fall and winter gatherings, or an easy vegetarian main course. We also like it with roast chicken stirred in for a heartier meal.

WILD RICE SALAD

1 small butternut squash, peeled, seeded, and cut into ½-inch cubes

1 yellow onion, thinly sliced

2 tablespoons olive oil, plus more for drizzling

½ teaspoon kosher salt, plus more for seasoning

½ teaspoon ground pepper, plus more for seasoning

½ teaspoon ground cumin

1 cup wild rice (see Note)

4 cups fresh arugula

1 cup pomegranate seeds

1 cup crumbled goat or feta cheese (about 4 ounces)

½ cup chopped fresh parsley

MAPLE MISO VINAIGRETTE

¼ cup apple cider or rice vinegar

2 tablespoons maple syrup

2 tablespoons white or yellow miso

1 tablespoon grated fresh ginger

¼ teaspoon kosher salt

½ cup olive oil

DIRECTIONS

1. **MAKE THE WILD RICE SALAD:** Preheat oven to 400°F. Spread the squash and onions on a rimmed baking sheet. Drizzle with 2 tablespoons olive oil and season with the salt, pepper, and cumin, then toss to coat. Roast until the squash is golden brown and the onions are softened, stirring halfway through, about 25 minutes. Set aside to cool.

2. Rinse the rice under cold water until the water runs clear. Add the rice to a medium saucepan with 3 cups water and a pinch of salt. Bring to a boil, then lower heat to simmer and cook, covered, for 25 to 40 minutes depending on the quality of your rice, until the water is absorbed.

3. **MAKE THE MAPLE MISO VINAIGRETTE:** Whisk the vinegar, maple syrup, miso, ginger, and salt together in a small bowl or jar until the miso is dissolved. Slowly pour in the olive oil, whisking constantly, until emulsified. Set aside.

4. Transfer the rice into a serving bowl. Let cool to room temperature, then add the squash, onions, and arugula. Season well with salt and pepper and drizzle with half of the dressing. Toss to combine and add more vinaigrette as desired. Sprinkle with pomegranate seeds, goat cheese, and parsley and serve immediately.

Note

The quality of wild rice varies widely, the best
being hand harvested in northern Minnesota
and Wisconsin. It's well worth the expense for
the difference in taste and texture—there's none
of the harsh aftertaste or hard grains you can
get in commercially harvested wild rice. I like to
purchase from Native Harvest (nativeharvest
.com), a collection of Ojibwe-made products
operated by the White Earth Land Recovery
Project. Their wild rice (or manoomin) is
hand harvested and wood parched by Ojibwe
tribal members using traditional methods.

Butternut Squash & Apple Soup

Serves 6 to 8

This lightly spiced soup is an ideal way to use an abundance of fall produce, and roasting the squash, apples, onions, and garlic before pureeing brings out their natural sweetness. I like to emphasize this even more by adding a little maple syrup, but you can omit it if you like. Either way, it's a tasty first course or light dinner all autumn long. We love it with crusty bread, but for an extra special dinner, serve it with Apple Gjetost Grilled Cheese (page 31) or your favorite grilled cheese recipe.

1 large butternut squash, cut in half lengthwise, seeds removed

¼ cup olive oil, plus more for drizzling

2 tablespoons maple syrup, plus more for drizzling

¼ teaspoon red pepper flakes

½ teaspoon kosher salt, plus more for seasoning

½ teaspoon ground pepper, plus more for seasoning

3 to 4 garlic cloves, unpeeled

2 apples, cored and cut into quarters

1 yellow onion, peeled and cut into quarters

2 cups vegetable or chicken broth

One 13.5-ounce can full-fat coconut milk

2 teaspoons chopped fresh thyme or rosemary, plus more for garnish

1-inch piece fresh ginger, grated

Sour cream or Greek yogurt for serving

DIRECTIONS

1. Preheat oven to 400°F. Line a rimmed baking sheet with parchment paper or foil.

2. Drizzle the squash halves with 2 tablespoons each of the olive oil and maple syrup, and season with the red pepper flakes and ½ teaspoon each of salt and pepper. Place the squash cut side down on the prepared baking sheet. Scatter the garlic, apples, and onion around the squash and drizzle with the remaining olive oil. Season with salt and pepper.

3. Roast the squash and apples until browned and very tender, about 40 minutes. Let cool until cool enough to handle, then remove the skin from the squash. Transfer the squash and apples to a blender. (If using a hand blender, transfer the squash and apples directly to a large pot, or Dutch oven.) Add the broth, coconut milk, thyme, and ginger. Use the blender or hand blender to puree the soup until smooth, 1 to 2 minutes. If using a blender, transfer the soup to a large pot or Dutch oven. Season to taste with salt and pepper, and warm over medium-low heat until hot, about 10 minutes.

4. To serve, sprinkle with fresh herbs, a dollop of sour cream, and a drizzle of olive oil and/or maple syrup.

Chicken Wild Rice Soup

Serves 6 to 8

Sometimes there's no need to mess with a classic. My mom often made a version of this soup (shared by her dear friend Caragh) during the long Minnesota winters when I was a kid, and there's nothing like a big, steaming bowl of it on a cold night. I like the texture that shredded chicken or turkey adds (and it's a great way to use up Thanksgiving leftovers), but it's also delicious with cubed ham or chopped bacon. If you like, stir in some more green vegetables at the end of the cooking time, such as frozen peas or chopped broccoli or spinach.

6 cups chicken stock

2 cups water

1¼ cups uncooked wild rice (see Note on page 65)

1 large leek, white and light green parts chopped, or 1 bunch green onions, chopped

8 ounces cremini or baby bella mushrooms, thinly sliced

4 carrots, thinly sliced into coins

¼ cup melted butter

¾ cup all-purpose flour

1 tablespoon kosher salt, plus more as needed

1 tablespoon ground pepper, plus more as needed

1½ cups half-and-half, warmed to about 100°F

2 cups cooked, shredded chicken or turkey (from a rotisserie chicken or roast chicken or turkey breasts or thighs)

¼ cup sherry or white wine

Fresh chopped chives and parsley, or tops of green onions, for garnish

DIRECTIONS

1. Place the chicken stock, water, wild rice, and leeks in a large stockpot or Dutch oven. Bring to a boil over high heat. Add the mushrooms and carrots and decrease the heat to low. Cover and simmer for 20 to 35 minutes, depending on the quality of your rice (you want it to be tender but with a bit of a bite).

2. Whisk the melted butter and flour together in a small bowl until no lumps remain. Whisk in about 1 cup of the hot soup broth about ¼ cup at a time until smooth.

3. When the rice is tender, stir in the flour mixture about ¼ cup at a time until incorporated. Season with salt and pepper. Gradually add the half-and-half a little at a time. Bring to a simmer over medium heat and cook until the soup is thickened, about 5 minutes. Stir in the chicken and sherry. Taste and add more salt and pepper as needed.

4. Serve with fresh chopped chives, parsley, or the tops of your green onions.

Smoked Trout Corn Chowder

Serves 4 to 6

Corn was undisputedly my favorite vegetable growing up, and I would happily have eaten Campbell's corn soup every day if I had been allowed. This version updates the classic creamy soup, adding a hint of smoke with cured trout—and if you want to be fancy, trout roe. It's best with peak-summer sweet corn—frozen won't taste the same. If you're not a fan of trout, substitute with 1 cup crumbled cooked bacon instead. For a vegetarian version, use vegetable broth and skip the trout altogether. Hot smoked salmon works well, too, if you can't find trout.

2 tablespoons butter

1 yellow onion, chopped

2 garlic cloves, minced

¼ cup flour

4 large dill sprigs, plus more for garnish

1 pound small Yukon Gold potatoes, cut into ½-inch coins

4 cups chicken or seafood stock

8 cups fresh corn kernels (from 6 ears corn)

8 ounces smoked trout, torn into bite-size pieces

1 cup buttermilk or Greek yogurt

½ teaspoon kosher salt, plus more as needed

½ teaspoon ground pepper

Trout roe (optional)

Thinly sliced radishes (optional)

DIRECTIONS

1. Melt the butter in a large Dutch oven or stockpot over medium heat. Add the onions and cook until they begin to brown, about 8 minutes.

2. Add the garlic and cook for 1 minute more. Stir in the flour and dill sprigs and cook for 1 minute. Add the potatoes and stock to the pot and bring to a boil. Turn down the heat to low and simmer until the potatoes are nearly fork tender, about 15 minutes. Add the corn and cook for another 5 to 10 minutes, until the potatoes and corn are tender.

3. Stir in the trout and buttermilk and cook until warmed through, about 3 minutes. Season with the salt and pepper, adding more if needed. Ladle into bowls and garnish with dill, trout roe, and radish slices, if using.

PASTA, GRAINS & BREADS

Strictly speaking, this chapter is mostly about hotdish.

To much of the United States, a hotdish is just a casserole, a humble, baked, one-pan dinner. And while this is true, it is also more than that: Traditionally a mix of protein, vegetable, starch, and creamed soup, hotdish was meant to be an easy one-dish meal for tired mothers, a stick-to-your-ribs kind of dinner for nights when the temperature falls to -20 degrees. It's brought to potlucks in backyards and church basements across the Midwest, or thrown together on busy nights after hockey practice by parents from Fargo to Milwaukee.

I grew up eating hotdish at large family gatherings or at dinner at my grandparents' houses, but I don't think I had actually ever attempted to make it before I started working on this cookbook. Maybe that makes me a questionable Minnesotan. But when I lived in New York in my early 20s, the ovens that came with my various apartments could barely fit a cake pan, let alone a full 9-by-13-inch baking dish. When I moved to California in 2015, I was so taken with all the incredible produce and diverse array of food that I rarely, if ever, cooked the nostalgic dishes from my childhood. And my husband, Ari, having grown up in Oakland, was not exactly craving hotdish when in need of comfort food—he's more inclined to seek out fried chicken or tacos.

Besides, I think hotdish is best enjoyed on a cold winter's night, when only a bowl filled with meat, cheese, and potatoes will do. For those kind of nights, Cheeseburger Hotdish (page 77) is an ideal balm, every bite a mixture of savory ground beef, cheesy sauce, and tender tater tots. And you can't go wrong with Chicken, Wild Rice & Butternut Squash Hotdish (page 78), an updated take on the creamy casserole. Making a homemade béchamel takes a little time but is well worth the effort, plus it's better for you than canned creamed soups as it lacks the preservatives and added sodium. Many of the hotdish recipes I found in my grandmothers' archives consisted of ground beef, canned vegetables, and tater tots, but the fact is, the combinations are endless: I stuck with spices and flavors common to traditional Minnesotan dishes, but if you can dream it up, you can make it. The state has grown more diverse and creative takes abound, from chaat-inspired hotdish to Hmong hotdish, which features additions like fresh shredded vegetables and Thai chiles. These recipes are shared in the local newspapers and by chefs around the region.

Of course, woman cannot live on hotdish alone, so to round things out this chapter provides recipes for a few simple breads (including foolproof Garlic-Chive Popovers, page 91, that come together in minutes) and Gjetost Mac & Cheese (page 81), which is a rather excellent take on baked mac and cheese with the Norwegian brown cheese gjetost and crispy rye bread crumbs.

Cheeseburger Hotdish

Serves 4

Sometimes only tater tots will do! This is the ultimate comfort food in one nostalgic dish, and it makes a perfect dinner on cold winter nights. I have also made it with vegetarian meat substitutes with great results, or you could try it with ground turkey or chicken for a lighter dish.

2 tablespoons olive oil

1 pound ground beef

½ cup chopped onion

¾ cup tomato sauce

1 tablespoon Dijon mustard

1 teaspoon Worcestershire sauce

1 teaspoon kosher salt

¼ teaspoon ground pepper

2 tablespoons unsalted butter

2 tablespoons all-purpose flour

1 cup milk, warmed

3 cups grated cheddar cheese (about 4 ounces)

1 pound frozen tater tots

¼ cup minced chives for garnish

DIRECTIONS

1. Preheat oven to 375°F.

2. Heat the olive oil in a 9- or 10-inch cast-iron skillet over medium heat. Add the ground beef and onions and cook until browned, about 10 minutes. Stir in the tomato sauce, mustard, Worcestershire, salt, and pepper. Remove from the heat and set aside.

3. Heat a saucepan over medium heat. Add the butter and cook until melted. Stir in the flour and cook, whisking constantly, until it begins to brown, about 2 minutes. Slowly whisk in the milk. Remove from the heat and whisk in the grated cheese.

4. Pour the cheese sauce over the hamburger mixture in the skillet. Tightly arrange the tater tots over the cheese sauce.

5. Bake for 40 to 50 minutes, until the filling is bubbling and the tater tots are golden brown. Let cool for a few minutes, then sprinkle with chives and serve.

Chicken, Wild Rice & Butternut Squash Hotdish

Serves 6 to 8

There's nothing like the combination of creamy wild rice and comforting chicken. Here, I add a butternut squash, swap the traditional canned soup for a homemade béchamel, and mix in tangy goat cheese for a creamy, comforting dinner—best enjoyed in front of a fire in the dead of winter. Serve with a crisp green salad.

1½ cups uncooked wild rice (see Note on page 65)

1 tablespoon kosher salt

2 small butternut squash, peeled, seeded, and cut in half lengthwise

1 tablespoon olive oil

5 tablespoons butter, plus more for baking dish

4 shallots or 2 medium yellow onions, chopped

1 tablespoon chopped fresh thyme

2 teaspoons chipotle chili powder

¼ cup flour

1 cup milk

1 cup half-and-half

2 cups chicken stock

½ cup crumbled goat cheese

2 teaspoons ground pepper

4 cups cooked, shredded chicken

DIRECTIONS

1. Rinse the rice under cold water until the water runs clear. Add the rice to a medium saucepan with 3½ cups water and a pinch of the salt. Bring to a boil, then lower heat to simmer and cook, covered, for 25 to 40 minutes depending on the quality of your rice, until the water is absorbed.

2. Meanwhile, preheat oven to 400°F. Slice the upper part of the butternut squash into ¼-inch-thick half moons. Set aside. Cut the base of the squash (the part that had seeds) into 1-inch cubes. Spread the cubes on a baking sheet and toss with the olive oil. Roast until lightly browned and tender, 20 to 25 minutes.

3. Reduce the oven to 375°F. Butter a 9-by-13-inch baking dish and set aside. Melt 4 tablespoons of the butter in a large skillet over medium heat. Add the shallots and cook until translucent and starting to brown, 8 to 10 minutes. Add the thyme and chipotle chili powder and stir until you can smell the aromatics, about a minute. Add the flour and stir until the shallots are coated. Add the milk and bring to a simmer, stirring constantly. Stir in the half-and-half, chicken stock, goat cheese, 2 teaspoons of the salt, and 1½ teaspoons of the pepper and cook over medium-high heat until slightly thickened, 5 to 8 minutes.

4. Stir in the shredded chicken, wild rice, and squash cubes. Spread the mixture in the prepared baking dish. Arrange the reserved squash slices over the chicken mixture. Melt the remaining tablespoon of butter and brush over the squash. Season with the remaining teaspoon of salt and ½ teaspoon of pepper. Bake until the squash slices are browned and the dish is heated through, 35 to 40 minutes.

Gjetost Mac & Cheese

Serves 6 to 8

This simple, kid-pleasing dinner comes together in under an hour. Using gjetost (Norwegian brown cheese) is highly recommended because it melts deliciously and adds pleasant, caramelized undertones to the cheddar sauce.

1 pound penne or medium-size shell pasta

¼ cup (½ stick) unsalted butter, plus more for baking dish

¼ cup all-purpose flour

2 cups milk, warmed

3 cups shredded sharp cheddar cheese (about 8 ounces)

1 cup shredded or shaved gjetost (about 4 ounces)

1½ teaspoons kosher salt

1 teaspoon ground mustard

½ teaspoon ground pepper

¼ teaspoon nutmeg

½ cup crushed Ritz crackers or Crispy Rye Bread Crumbs (page 59)

DIRECTIONS

1. Preheat oven to 400°F. Butter a 9-by-13-inch baking dish. Cook the pasta until al dente according to package directions. Drain and set aside.

2. Melt the butter in a large skillet over medium heat. Whisk in the flour and cook until beginning to brown, stirring constantly, 2 to 3 minutes.

3. Gradually add the milk, whisking after each addition. Cook until the sauce begins to thicken, about 5 minutes. Stir in the cheeses, salt, ground mustard, pepper, and nutmeg and whisk until the sauce is smooth and creamy.

4. Stir the pasta into the sauce until well coated. Transfer to the prepared baking dish and spread in an even layer. Sprinkle with Ritz crackers or Crispy Rye Bread Crumbs. Bake until the topping is golden brown and the cheese is bubbling, 25 to 30 minutes.

5. Serve immediately.

Note

To add in some greens, stir in 2 to 4 cups vegetables of your choosing, such as cauliflower, broccoli florets, or frozen peas before baking.

Ham & Potato Hotdish

Serves 6 to 8

Think of this like a hotdish version of a croque monsieur (one of the all-time greatest sandwiches, it must be said). Tender potatoes, smoked ham, caramelized onions, and a creamy sauce are combined in one pan for a hearty winter meal. You could also try it topped with fried eggs for a rich brunch dish!

2 tablespoons butter, plus more to coat pan

2 large yellow onions, thinly sliced

3 pounds russet or Yukon Gold potatoes, peeled and cut into ¼-inch-thick slices

Kosher salt

Ground pepper

¾ pound sliced smoked ham

4 cups grated Gruyère, Jarlsberg, or Swiss cheese (about 6 ounces)

1 cup whole milk

1 cup chicken broth

1 tablespoon Dijon mustard

1 tablespoon flour

1 tablespoon fresh thyme leaves, plus more for serving

¼ teaspoon nutmeg

DIRECTIONS

1. Coat a 9-by-13-inch baking pan with butter or baking spray.

2. Preheat oven to 375°F. Melt the butter in a large skillet over medium-low heat. Add the onions and cook until deeply browned and caramelized, stirring often, about 45 minutes. Don't rush this step!

3. Layer one-third of the potatoes over the bottom of the prepared pan. Season with salt and pepper. Spread with one-half of the caramelized onions. Place half of the ham slices over the potatoes, then sprinkle with 1½ cups of the cheese. Repeat with another one-third of the potatoes, then remaining onions, ham, and 1½ cups cheese. Spread the remaining one-third of the potatoes on top and season with salt and pepper.

4. Whisk the milk, broth, mustard, flour, thyme, and nutmeg together in a small saucepan over medium heat. Cook until the flour dissolves and the mixture starts to thicken, about 5 minutes. Pour the sauce over the potatoes in the baking dish.

5. Sprinkle the remaining cheese over the potatoes. Bake until the potatoes are very tender and the hotdish is bubbling, about 1 hour. Uncover and bake until the cheese browns, about 30 minutes more. Cool for 20 minutes. Sprinkle with fresh thyme and cut into squares and serve.

On Lefse

Although lefse is among the most popular of the Scandinavian foods my ancestors brought over from Norway when they settled in the United States, it's not one I had ever attempted to make until recently. My sister Annelise, cousin Kari, and aunt Mary are master lefse makers, and their silky, tender pancakes are a far cry from the tough and sometimes mealy product you can buy at the grocery store come winter in Minnesota.

Like many traditional foods, such as handmade pasta, dumplings, or laminated croissant dough, making lefse is not an easy or fast endeavor. The first time I made lefse, Kari showed my mom and sisters and me how to roll out the delicate dough using a grooved lefse rolling pin, and how to cook it on the electric griddle. The second time I made it was several years later as I was writing this book, alone in my kitchen with memories of that day and the internet to guide me. The results were fine, but nothing special. The dough tore easily, I overcooked many of the pancakes, and while the taste wasn't bad, it wasn't really good either.

Since then, I've done more research. I made it with my mom on a hot July afternoon, and we talked about the many Scandinavian desserts that require both time and effort: delicate krumkake cookies that are cooked on a griddle and rolled one by one, temperamental fried rosettes doused in sugar, and of course lefse, the fragile potato dough liable to tear if you don't use enough flour or exert too much force. I imagined my ancestors, grandmothers and great-grandmothers, sturdy farmers' wives and daughters, as they gathered over wood-burning stoves in drafty farmhouses while they gossiped and cut and rolled and cooked and created these delicacies one by one over many hours. For these women, the gatherings must have had dual purposes—not only were they preparing holiday treats for their families, but it was also a chance to catch up on news from neighbors and to enjoy the company of other women. No doubt there was always a pot of strong coffee close at hand. Later, the stoves and griddles were powered by gas and electricity, but the purpose of the gatherings would have remained the same.

My lefse-making skills are still a work in progress (and I have a feeling they will take many more hours to hone), but it didn't take me long to grasp a central tenet of cooking these humble pancakes: It's a task best shared with family and friends, a communal effort. While one person forms the dough into patties, one rolls, and one cooks, and any frustration brought on by tearing dough or an overcooked pancake is soon forgotten by the pleasure of company.

Although you don't necessarily need a special cloth-covered board, rolling pin, and lefse griddle to make them, they certainly help the process run more smoothly. I use my regular rolling pin and cast-iron skillet in a pinch (and plenty of flour to help keep the dough from sticking). And while I'm not sure if it's something I'll undertake every year during the holidays, I know that making lefse is a tradition that will live on in our family as long as there's someone who's willing to make the effort.

Lefse

Makes about 30

Lefse—mashed potato flatbread—is ubiquitous in Minnesota around the holiday season. My sister, cousin, and aunt are masters at creating thin, lacy rounds. In my family, lefse is traditionally served with butter and sugar, but these days I like it with sliced ham and cheese, or sour cream and smoked salmon, like latkes. This recipe was adapted from a recipe by my Ellingboe cousins' Grandma Delores, who made the best lefse I have ever encountered. Serve as desired, with butter and sugar, jam, meat and cheese, or smoked salmon.

5 cups chilled mashed russet potatoes (from about 3 pounds)

½ cup heavy whipping cream

⅓ cup melted butter

1 teaspoon kosher salt

1 teaspoon sugar (optional)

2 cups flour, plus more for rolling

DIRECTIONS

1. Place mashed potatoes in a large bowl. Add the cream, butter, salt, and sugar (if using) and mash together to mix. Cover with plastic wrap and refrigerate until cold, at least 30 minutes and up to 1 day.

2. When cold, divide the dough in half. Place one-half in a bowl and add 1 cup of the flour. Knead until very smooth, about 2 minutes. Form into 2- to 3-inch patties and place on a rimmed baking sheet. Cover with plastic wrap. Place the patties in the refrigerator and repeat with the remaining half of the dough.

3. When ready to cook, dust your work surface liberally with flour. Heat a large dry skillet or lefse griddle over high heat. Roll one patty at a time from the center out as thin as you can, about ⅛ inch thick. The lefse is considered very good when you hold it up and can see light through it. If you have a cloth-covered board and lefse rolling pin, now is the time to use them—the cloth helps prevent the delicate dough from sticking. If you don't have a cloth-covered board, you will need to use a lot of flour. Be sure to brush some of the flour off of the lefse before cooking so they don't burn.

4. Place the rolled lefse in the pan and cook until just beginning to speckle with light brown spots, about 1 minute. Flip with a turning stick or spatula and cook 30 seconds more. Transfer the cooked lefse to a plate.

5. Repeat with remaining patties.

6. Lefse can be covered and refrigerated for up to 1 week, or stacked between parchment paper and frozen for up to 3 months.

Note

For best results, use a cloth-covered board and a grooved lefse rolling pin to roll out the lefse, an electric griddle to cook it, and a wooden turner to flip it, all of which you can purchase online. However, you can also use a regular rolling pin, cutting board or stone, and skillet. Just be sure to coat everything liberally with flour and keep the dough well chilled as you make it.

Norwegian Rye Bread

Makes two 8-inch loaves

Also known as rugbrød, this Scandinavian-style hearty bread is denser and darker than what you'll find at the grocery store (typically a Jewish-style rye), and it uses caraway seeds for flavor and earthy rye flour for depth. Toasting the spices is an extra step, but it's worth it for the added flavor. Use this bread for the open-face sandwiches in a Smorgasbord (page 175), popular in Norway and Sweden, or slather with butter and flaky salt for a simple breakfast or snack.

2 teaspoons caraway seeds

1 teaspoon fennel seeds

½ teaspoon aniseed or fenugreek seeds

2 packages (2¼ teaspoons each) active dry yeast

1 cup warm (110°F) milk

1½ cups all-purpose flour

1 teaspoon sugar

1 cup warm (110°F) water

4½ cups rye flour

3 tablespoons dark, unsulphured molasses

3 tablespoons butter, melted

2 teaspoons kosher salt

1 teaspoon white vinegar

DIRECTIONS

1. Heat a small skillet over medium heat. Add the caraway seeds, fennel seeds, and aniseed and toast until fragrant, 1 to 2 minutes. Remove from the skillet and grind with a spice grinder or mortar and pestle.

2. Place the yeast in a glass measuring cup. Add the milk and let sit for 5 minutes, until foamy. Combine the all-purpose flour and sugar in the bowl of a stand mixer. Add the yeast mixture and let stand for 5 minutes. Add the water, rye flour, molasses, butter, salt, vinegar, and toasted spices. Mix with a dough hook on low speed until combined.

3. Increase the speed to medium and mix until the dough is smooth and pulls away from the side of the bowl, about 5 minutes. Alternatively, turn the dough onto a lightly floured surface and knead by hand until smooth and elastic, 5 to 10 minutes. It will still be a bit sticky.

4. Lightly coat a large bowl with oil. Transfer the dough to the bowl, turning to coat all sides. Cover with a cloth and let rise until doubled, about 1 hour. Punch down the dough, return it to a floured surface, and knead until the dough is no longer sticky, about 2 minutes.

5. Preheat oven to 400°F. Line two rimmed baking sheets with parchment paper. Divide the dough in half and shape into two 8-inch-round or oval loaves on the prepared baking sheets. Cover each loaf with a dishcloth and let rise for 1 hour.

6. Bake until the crust is well browned and hardened, 30 to 40 minutes. Cool on a rack.

Flatbrød

Makes about 16 large crackers

These simple crackers are a very old dish in Norway, and have been a staple in Scandinavian cuisine for hundreds of years. This recipe was adapted from the Sons of Norway, a Minnesotan cultural organization, and these crackers are served with everything from pickled herring to soft cheese to butter and jam. Substitute butter for the lard if you're vegetarian or don't like lard.

1½ cups all-purpose flour, plus more for rolling

½ cup rye flour

1 teaspoon kosher salt

¾ teaspoon baking soda

¼ teaspoon ground pepper

1 cup buttermilk

½ cup leaf lard, melted

DIRECTIONS

1. Preheat oven to 350°F. Whisk the all-purpose flour, rye flour, salt, baking soda, and pepper together in a large bowl. Add the buttermilk and lard and stir to combine. The dough should be stiff but not sticky.

2. Lightly dust your work surface and a rolling pin with flour. Divide the dough into four pieces. Roll one piece of dough at a time as thin as you possibly can, until slightly transparent. Dust with more flour if needed so that the dough doesn't stick. Cut the dough into four to six large pieces and transfer to a rimmed baking sheet. Repeat with the remaining dough. Crackers should not touch. You may need more than one baking sheet.

3. Bake for about 8 minutes, flipping halfway through if needed, until crisp and golden brown on both sides.

Note

High-quality leaf lard adds a delicious flaky texture to these crackers. Find it at your local butcher shop or the meat section of your grocery store.

Garlic-Chive Popovers

Makes 6

I always thought popovers were intimidating before encountering this recipe, but I'm happy to report that not only are they incredibly easy to prepare, but you also probably already have everything on hand to make them! While the garlic-chive butter isn't strictly necessary, you're going to want to make it so you can slather it on everything.

GARLIC-CHIVE BUTTER

¼ cup unsalted butter, softened

2 garlic cloves, minced

2 tablespoons minced chives

¼ teaspoon kosher salt

POPOVERS

1 cup flour

1 cup whole or 2% milk, room temperature

4 eggs, room temperature

1 teaspoon kosher salt

DIRECTIONS

1. **MAKE GARLIC-CHIVE BUTTER:** Mix the butter, garlic, chives, and salt together in a small bowl until well combined.

2. Preheat oven to 450°F. Butter a 6-cup muffin tin or popover pan and place on a rimmed baking sheet. If using a 12-cup muffin tin, butter every other cup so that the popovers bake evenly.

3. **MAKE THE POPOVERS:** In a medium bowl, whisk the flour and milk together for 1 minute, until frothy. You want to add a lot of air so that the popovers will rise! Add about 1 tablespoon of the garlic-chive butter and whisk to combine. Reserve the remaining garlic-chive butter. Add the eggs, one at a time, whisking after each addition. Stir in the salt.

4. Divide the batter between the muffin cups (they will be full). Bake for 20 minutes.

5. Decrease oven temperature to 350°F. Bake for an additional 15 to 20 minutes, until the popovers are puffed and golden brown.

6. Immediately remove the popovers from the pan. Serve warm with the remaining garlic-chive butter.

Speedy Homemade Rolls

Makes about 30

I don't always take the time to make homemade rolls, but I never regret it when I do. These easy rolls only require one rise, and their tender crumb is ideal for ham sandwiches or as part of your Thanksgiving spread (or simply with peanut butter and jelly!).

1 cup water

1 cup milk

Three ¼-ounce packages active
   dry yeast (6¾ teaspoons)

¼ cup sugar

1 tablespoon kosher salt

2 eggs

6 tablespoons (¾ stick) butter, melted,
   plus more for brushing

6½ cups flour

Flaky sea salt, such as Maldon

DIRECTIONS

1. Place the water and milk in a small saucepan. Heat over medium to 115°F. Do not boil. Remove from the heat and add the yeast. Let sit for 10 minutes, until the yeast dissolves and begins to foam.

2. Add the milk-yeast mixture to the bowl of a stand mixer. Add the sugar, salt, eggs, melted butter, and ½ cup of the flour. Whisk to combine. Attach the bowl to the mixer, fitted with the dough hook. With the mixer on low, gradually add the remaining flour until the dough is smooth and pulls away from the side of the bowl. Increase the speed to medium and mix for 5 minutes, until the dough is smooth and not very sticky.

3. Transfer to a lightly oiled bowl and cover with plastic wrap. Rest in a warm place until doubled in volume, about 40 minutes to 1 hour.

4. Preheat oven to 375°F. Line two rimmed baking sheets with parchment paper.

5. Punch down the dough and transfer to a lightly floured work surface. Divide the dough in half, then cut each half into quarters. Cut each quarter into three to four pieces (you should have around 30 total). Roll one piece into a ball and, pulling from the sides, pinch the dough together like a dumpling a few times onto the bottom. Place the pinched side down onto the prepared baking sheet (this ensures a nice, round shape and smooth top). Repeat with all remaining pieces. Space the rolls 2 inches apart.

6. Bake until the rolls are puffed and golden brown, about 20 minutes. Brush the warm rolls with butter and sprinkle with flaky salt.

7. Serve immediately, or store covered at room temperature for up to 3 days. Alternatively, freeze for up to 3 months.

Spring Vegetable Hotdish/Potpie

Serves 6

Is a potpie technically a hotdish? With protein, vegetables, and a creamy sauce topped by starch, I think it fits the bill. Typically, radishes are consumed raw, but roasting them brings out their natural sweetness and adds nice texture to this vegetable-forward dish. You can also use carrots cut into coins, or add 2 cups shredded chicken or turkey. I also love this one-pot meal topped with tater tots instead of pie dough!

¼ cup unsalted butter

1 leek, white and light green parts thinly sliced (see Note), or 1 medium yellow onion, chopped

12 ounces cremini mushrooms, cut into quarters

¼ cup flour

2 cups vegetable or chicken stock, warmed

1 cup half-and-half, warmed

1½ cups fresh or frozen peas

1 bunch asparagus, trimmed and cut into 1-inch pieces (about 1 pound)

1 bunch radishes, trimmed and quartered, greens reserved and chopped (about 6 ounces)

1 teaspoon ground pepper

Kosher salt

1 disc store-bought or homemade pie dough (Piecrust, page 216), or one 7- to 8-ounce-sheet frozen puff pastry, thawed

1 egg, lightly beaten

DIRECTIONS

1. Preheat oven to 425°F. Melt the butter in a 9- or 10-inch ovenproof skillet over medium heat.

2. Add the leeks to the skillet and cook until tender, about 5 minutes. Add the mushrooms and cook until browned, 8 to 10 minutes.

3. Whisk the flour into the leek mixture and cook, stirring often, until golden brown and nutty, 2 to 3 minutes.

4. Add the stock and scrape up the browned bits from the pan. Add the half-and-half and bring to a simmer. Cook until the mixture is thickened and coats the back of a spoon, about 10 minutes. Stir in the peas, asparagus, radishes, greens, and pepper. Taste and add salt as needed.

5. Roll the pie dough into a 10- to 11-inch circle and drape over the vegetable mixture, tucking the edges around the sides of the pan. Brush with the egg wash. Cut several slits into the dough to allow air to escape.

6. Place the skillet on a rimmed baking sheet. Bake for 30 to 40 minutes, until the pastry is golden brown and the vegetables are tender. Let cool for 10 minutes before serving.

Note

Nothing is worse than grit in your teeth from sandy leeks! To make sure they are thoroughly cleaned, soak the sliced leeks in a bowl of water for 10 minutes. Drain, rinse, and soak again. Repeat again as needed until no sand falls to the bottom of the bowl. Dry with a dishcloth and cook away!

VEGETABLES,
SIDES & PICKLES

We're a potato family.

Ari and I will happily eat potatoes in nearly any form (except crinkle cut fries, which are rubbish). Luckily, my ancestors and fellow Midwesterners are in agreement about the importance of the humble potato. Whether fried French-style (Aquavit Moules Frites, page 129), smothered in sour cream and chilled (Sour Cream Potato Salad, page 119), or baked with milk and cheese until tender (Scalloped Potatoes, page 117), potatoes lend themselves to many different (and delicious) preparations and go with pretty much every savory dish.

In addition to potatoes, I'm always craving a variety of textures and flavors in any given meal, so side dishes are essential. From crisp green beans to creamy Scalloped Corn (page 106), the dishes in this chapter are meant to complement any main dish, from slow-roasted fish to chicken tenders to grilled burgers.

Though I now find acidity an essential part of any balanced meal, I didn't really like pickles when I was a kid. Maybe it was because my experience was limited to sour dill pickles (still not my favorite), but I could take them or leave them well into adulthood. However, I do remember the first time I tried quick pickles—their bright crunch was a different thing altogether than the store-bought spears I was used to. As was typical for most farm families, my ancestors were no stranger to pickles and preserves, their briny goodness livening up bland winter meals and extending the freshness of summer cucumbers, corn, and carrots well past their limited growing season.

I started making quick pickled cucumbers and onions in my 20s to liven up tacos, salads, and sandwiches, but it wasn't until I started working on this book that I really began to appreciate their versatility and variety. In fact, while writing this book I made Refrigerator Pickles (page 113) more than any other recipe because we go through jars so quickly. I usually just store them in the fridge, but any of the pickles made from the recipes in this chapter can be preserved for the long term—I typically follow the instructions in the *Ball Blue Book Guide to Preserving*.

Green Beans & Snap Peas with Buttermilk Herb Dressing

Serves 6 to 8

Blanching the green beans and peas in this bright salad keeps them super crisp and maintains their bright green color, and by mixing them with fresh snap peas, you obtain an ideal mix of snappy textures. All the components for this dish can be made ahead of time, making it an ideal side dish for potlucks or other casual gatherings.

1 red onion, thinly sliced

1 pound green beans, trimmed and cut into 1-inch pieces

2 cups fresh or frozen peas

1 pound snap peas, trimmed and thinly sliced on the bias

Kosher salt

Ground pepper

1 cup Buttermilk Herb Dressing (page 62), plus more as needed

Fresh chopped parsley or tarragon for garnish

DIRECTIONS

1. Fill a small bowl with ice water. Place the onions in the water and let sit for 10 minutes. Drain, then set aside.

2. Fill a large bowl with ice water. Bring a large pot of water to a boil. Add the green beans and frozen peas and cook until bright green and crisp, about 2 minutes. Drain and immediately transfer to the ice water.

3. Dry the onions and green beans with a dishcloth. Place in a large serving bowl. Add the snap peas and season with salt and pepper. Drizzle with Buttermilk Herb Dressing and toss well to mix. Garnish with the fresh herbs and serve immediately.

4. **MAKE AHEAD:** You can blanch and mix the vegetables up to 1 day ahead. Cover and refrigerate, and mix with the dressing just before serving.

Grilled Corn with Dill Butter

Serves 6

Prime summer sweet corn needs no adornment, but if you find yourself with less than peak-season corn, or are simply looking to switch things up, this simple compound butter is a lovely accompaniment. If you want the full Midwestern experience, be sure to buy your corn from an honor-system roadside farm stand on a humid day in August, then grill immediately when you get home, slathering the cobs in butter and salt. If you're not a fan of dill, this is equally delicious with other herbs, such as basil, parsley, cilantro, or thyme, or a mix of your favorites.

½ cup (1 stick) unsalted butter, room temperature

2 garlic cloves, minced

2 tablespoons minced dill

1 tablespoon lemon zest

1 teaspoon kosher salt, plus more if needed

½ teaspoon ground pepper, plus more if needed

6 ears corn

DIRECTIONS

1. Mix the butter, garlic, dill, lemon zest, salt, and pepper in a small bowl until well combined. Set aside if grilling corn immediately, or cover and refrigerate for up to 1 day.

2. Preheat the grill to medium-high. Grill the corn in their husks (no need to soak), until the husks are charred and softened, about 10 minutes. If desired, remove the husks and grill corn for a few minutes more, until the kernels begin to char.

3. Transfer the corn to a large plate. Slather with the butter on all sides and season with additional salt and pepper if needed. Serve immediately.

Sautéed Cucumbers

Serves 6 to 8

I first remember hearing about cooked cucumbers as being "a revelation" in the movie *Julie & Julia,* with the original recipe coming, of course, from Julia Child's iconic book *Mastering the Art of French Cooking.* While the classic French preparation simply uses butter, salt, lemon juice, and a pinch of dried mint, this recipe adds a Nordic twist with the addition of dill and coriander. I love to serve this dish with Caraway Roast Chicken (page 125) or Slow-Roasted Trout with Citrus & Fennel (page 135). They also make a delicious and unexpected appetizer.

2 medium cucumbers, peeled
   and sliced ¼ inch thick

1½ teaspoons kosher salt

6 tablespoons all-purpose flour

½ teaspoon pepper

1 teaspoon minced fresh dill

½ teaspoon ground coriander

2 tablespoons butter

DIRECTIONS

1. Place the cucumbers and salt in a medium bowl and stir to coat. Transfer to a colander and place the colander over the bowl. Let sit for 30 minutes. Dry the cucumbers thoroughly with a dishcloth or paper towels.

2. After 30 minutes, combine the flour, pepper, dill, and coriander in a large bowl.

3. Melt the butter in a large skillet over medium-high heat. Working in batches, add about one-quarter of the cucumbers to the flour mixture and toss to coat. Cook the cucumbers until golden brown and crisp, about 30 seconds to 1 minute per side. Remove the cucumbers to a rack. Repeat with the remaining cucumbers. Serve immediately.

Scalloped Corn

Serves 6

There is an abundance of corn recipes in this book, and that's because it's one of my favorite vegetables (especially peak-summer sweet corn straight from the field, but I have a soft spot for canned corn, too). While some of the other recipes in this book make the most of that all-too-short prime summer corn season, this easy side is a great way to make use of cobs that may be a little more . . . lackluster. No matter what the season, fresh corn is irresistible when combined with milk and eggs and topped with crunchy Ritz crackers (don't skip those). You can make it with frozen corn as well—use 5 to 6 cups.

4 ears corn, husks and silk removed

2 eggs, lightly beaten

1 cup whole milk

3 tablespoons butter, melted

1 tablespoon chopped fresh thyme, plus more for garnish

1 teaspoon kosher salt

½ teaspoon ground pepper

1 cup crushed Ritz crackers

DIRECTIONS

1. Preheat oven to 350°F. Butter a 9- or 10-inch round or square baking dish.

2. Use a serrated knife to cut the corn kernels from the cobs. Place the kernels in a large bowl. Add the eggs, milk, butter, thyme, salt, and pepper and stir until completely combined.

3. Transfer to the prepared baking dish and sprinkle with the Ritz crackers. Bake until golden brown and the center is set but still jiggly, 25 to 30 minutes.

4. Cool for 10 minutes and garnish with additional thyme if desired. Serve warm or at room temperature.

Corn Relish

Makes 3 to 4 pints

The original recipe for this savory relish from my great-grandma Soberg's archives called for 18 (!) ears of corn, and green peppers instead of jalapeños and was clearly meant to preserve summer sweet corn through the winter. I'm not a fan of green peppers, but if you are, add 1 diced green or red pepper to the onion and cabbage in step 2. If you're not using peak-summer sweet corn, add another ¼ cup sugar to the brine.

6 ears corn

1½ cups white vinegar

½ cup water

¼ cup sugar

1 tablespoon mustard seeds

1 teaspoon kosher salt

1 white onion, chopped

¼ green cabbage, chopped

1 jalapeño, sliced into rings (optional)

DIRECTIONS

1. Remove the corn husks, silk, and ends of cobs. Use a serrated knife to cut the kernels from the cob.

2. Combine the vinegar, water, sugar, mustard seeds, and salt in a large saucepan over medium heat. Bring to a simmer and stir until the sugar dissolves. Add the onion and cabbage and cook for 5 minutes, or until beginning to soften. Add the corn and jalapeños and cook for 2 minutes, or until tender.

3. If canning the relish, transfer it to sterilized jars and process according to directions in the *Ball Blue Book Guide to Preserving* or on freshpreserving.com. Alternatively, relish will keep in the refrigerator for 4 to 6 weeks.

Opposite page, from left: **Corn Relish, Refrigerator Pickles (page 113), and Mixed Pickled Vegetables (page 112)**

Pickled Cherry Tomatoes

Makes 2 pints

Pickled tomatoes are an unexpected but delicious condiment when served as part of a cheese plate, on sandwiches, or for a pop of acidity in salads. They're particularly tasty on toast spread with goat or cream cheese and sprinkled with herbs. I found that I like these best when eaten within a couple of weeks of pickling, otherwise the vinegar becomes a bit overwhelming.

2 pints cherry tomatoes

1 shallot, thinly sliced

1 tablespoon coriander seeds

1 tablespoon black peppercorns

1 cup white vinegar

½ cup water

½ cup sugar

2 tablespoons kosher salt

DIRECTIONS

1. Divide the tomatoes, shallots, coriander seeds, and peppercorns between clean jars.

2. Place the vinegar, water, sugar, and salt in a small saucepan. Bring to a simmer over medium heat, stirring until the sugar and salt have dissolved.

3. Pour the vinegar mixture over the tomatoes. Let cool, then cover and refrigerate for at least 1 hour and up to 2 weeks.

Opposite page, from left: **Pickled Cherry Tomatoes and Refrigerator Pickles (page 113)**

Mixed Pickled Vegetables

Makes 3 quarts

This recipe was found in my grandma Veola's files. I love to serve these with an outdoor lunch of sandwich fixings, potato salad, and chilled wine. You can change up the mix of vegetables for what you have on hand—try green beans, bell peppers, asparagus, or cabbage.

4 cups white vinegar

2 cups water

1 cup sugar

¼ cup kosher salt

4 carrots, peeled and cut into ½-inch sticks

4 garlic cloves, peeled

3 Persian cucumbers, cut lengthwise into spears

3 celery stalks, cut into ½-inch sticks

2 Fresno chiles, thinly sliced, or 1 red pepper, thinly sliced

1 small yellow onion, peeled and cut into rings

½ head cauliflower, stalk removed and cut into florets (reserve remainder for other use)

2 teaspoons mustard seeds

2 teaspoons whole peppercorns

DIRECTIONS

1. Place the white vinegar, water, sugar, and salt in a large saucepan. Bring to a boil over high heat, stirring until the sugar dissolves. Remove from the heat and let cool completely.

2. Divide the vegetables, mustard seeds, and peppercorns between sterilized jars. Pour the pickling liquid over the vegetables, filling to ½ inch below the rim. Attach lids.

3. If canning, process according to canning directions in the *Ball Blue Book Guide to Preserving* or on freshpreserving.com. Alternatively, refrigerate for at least 1 day and up to 6 weeks.

Refrigerator Pickles

Makes 4 pints

The original storage instructions for these quick pickles were "Put in refrigerator and keeps for a while." This was one of the recipes that I found myself making again and again while writing this book—they are the perfect combination of crisp, tart, and sweet and can easily be halved or quartered, depending on how much you want to make. I love them with sandwiches of all kinds or as part of a cheese board.

8 cups thinly sliced English cucumbers (from about 2 large)

1 cup thinly sliced white or yellow onions (from 1 small)

1 tablespoon celery seeds

1 tablespoon black peppercorns

2 cups white vinegar

1 cup water

1 cup sugar

¼ cup kosher salt

DIRECTIONS

1. Divide the cucumbers, onions, celery seeds, and peppercorns between clean jars.

2. Place the vinegar, water, sugar, and salt in a small saucepan. Bring to a simmer over medium heat, stirring until the sugar and salt have dissolved.

3. Pour the vinegar mixture over the cucumbers. Let cool, then cover and refrigerate for at least 1 hour and up to 6 weeks.

Rhubarb Compote

Makes about 2½ cups

Rhubarb is everywhere in the Midwest in early spring, and its tart flavor is incredible in both desserts and savory applications. I always chop up some stalks and freeze them to have on hand year-round, but I also love this easy compote to preserve that pure rhubarb flavor. Vanilla and rhubarb make for a wonderful pairing, but you could also try this with a tablespoon of minced fresh ginger and a little orange zest, or for a different take throw in a couple of fresh bay leaves and a teaspoon of lemon zest.

1 pound chopped rhubarb (about 4 cups)
½ to ¾ cup sugar
1 vanilla bean (see Note)

DIRECTIONS

1. Place the rhubarb and sugar in a large saucepan. Use a sharp knife to cut the vanilla bean in half lengthwise. Using the knife, scrape the vanilla seeds into the pan, then add the pods. Stir to coat with the sugar. Bring to a simmer, then reduce the heat to medium-low. Cook, stirring to dissolve the sugar, until the rhubarb is very soft and the mixture begins to gel, 15 to 20 minutes. Remove vanilla bean pods and discard.

2. If canning, cool, transfer to sterilized jars, and process as directed in the *Ball Blue Book Guide to Preserving* or on freshpreserving.com. Alternatively, refrigerate in clean jars for up to 1 month. This compote is delicious spread on toast or stirred into yogurt or ice cream.

Note

While a whole vanilla bean imparts wonderful flavor to this compote, they are pricey! You can substitute 2 teaspoons vanilla paste or high-quality vanilla extract instead.

Cheesy Potatoes

Serves 10 to 12

This shredded potato casserole is adapted from my grandma Nancy's recipe, and versions of it are a staple at funerals and church potlucks across the Midwest (as well as at my extended family's annual Christmas Day gathering). To save time, you can also use frozen, thawed hash browns. Serve alongside ham sandwiches for lunch or as a delicious (and rich) brunch side with scrambled eggs and bacon or sausage.

2 cups chicken broth

2 cups milk

½ cup flour

¼ cup chopped fresh chives, plus more for garnish

½ teaspoon garlic powder

½ teaspoon onion powder

½ teaspoon kosher salt, plus more to taste

½ teaspoon ground pepper, plus more to taste

2 cups grated cheddar cheese

1 cup sour cream

1 small yellow onion, chopped

3 pounds russet potatoes, peeled

½ cup (1 stick) unsalted butter

2½ cups cornflakes

DIRECTIONS

1. Preheat oven to 350°F.

2. Place the chicken broth and ½ cup of the milk in a small saucepan over medium heat. Bring to a simmer.

3. Meanwhile, whisk ½ cup of the milk, flour, chives, garlic powder, onion powder, ½ teaspoon salt, and ½ teaspoon pepper together in a small bowl. Add to the broth in the pan and whisk until combined.

4. Simmer, stirring frequently until thickened, about 8 minutes. Set aside to cool slightly.

5. Mix the broth mixture with the cheddar cheese, sour cream, and onion. Season with salt and pepper.

6. Shred the potatoes in a food processor or box grater. Transfer the potatoes to a dishcloth and squeeze until almost completely dry.

7. Transfer to a large bowl and season with salt. Add the chicken broth mixture and stir to coat.

8. Melt 4 tablespoons of the butter in the microwave or a small saucepan. Pour over the bottom of a 9-by-13-inch baking dish. Set aside.

9. Spread the hash brown mixture over the butter and season with salt and pepper.

10. Melt the remaining 4 tablespoons butter in the microwave or a small saucepan. Mix with the cornflakes. Sprinkle the cornflakes in an even layer over the top of the potatoes and season with salt.

11. Bake for 1½ hours, until the topping is golden brown and the potatoes are bubbling. Serve immediately.

Scalloped Potatoes

Serves 6 to 8

Scalloped potatoes are a staple at many of my family gatherings, and the original recipes in my grandmothers' archives were simplicity itself: They were basically just sliced potatoes covered in milk, seasoned with salt, and baked until tender. I find using russet potatoes works best thanks to their high starch content, though you could substitute sliced zucchini for some of the potatoes for a different take. This rich side is a favorite served with Caraway Roast Chicken (page 125) or with Maple-Glazed Ham (page 189) instead of mashed potatoes on Thanksgiving. Alternatively, include it as part of an Easter or springtime lunch spread.

4 tablespoons (½ stick) butter,
plus more for baking dish

1 yellow onion, finely chopped

2 garlic cloves, minced

¼ cup all-purpose flour

1 teaspoon kosher salt

½ teaspoon ground pepper

3 cups milk, warmed to 110°F to 120°F

4 pounds russet potatoes, peeled
and cut into ½-inch slices

½ cup chopped parsley, plus more for garnish

1 cup grated Gruyère, Jarlsberg, or Swiss cheese

DIRECTIONS

1. Preheat oven to 350°F. Butter a 9-by-13-inch or 2-quart baking dish.

2. Melt the butter in a small saucepan over medium heat. Add the onions and cook until softened and beginning to brown, about 10 minutes. Add the garlic and cook for 1 minute more. Stir in the flour, salt, and pepper and cook for 1 minute. Add the milk ½ cup at a time and simmer until the mixture begins to thicken, about 5 minutes. Remove from the heat.

3. Spread the potatoes in an even layer in the prepared pan and sprinkle with the parsley. Pour the milk mixture over the potatoes, then sprinkle with the cheese. Cover with aluminum foil.

4. Bake for about 25 minutes, until beginning to bubble. Remove the cover and bake for 20 to 30 minutes more, until the potatoes are very tender and the cheese is browned and bubbly.

5. Serve immediately, or cover and keep warm for up to 1 hour.

Garlic-Chive Mashed Potatoes

Serves 4 to 6

I know, you probably don't need another mashed potato recipe—but trust me, you want this one. Using flavorful Yukon Golds and plenty of garlic means that these potatoes hold their own as part of any meal. Use any leftovers for Norwegian Potato Balls (page 40) or Mashed Potato Pancakes (page 8)!

2 pounds Yukon Gold potatoes, peeled if desired and cut into 1-inch pieces

1 tablespoon kosher salt, plus more for cooking water

½ cup (1 stick) unsalted butter

4 garlic cloves, minced

1 cup whole milk, warmed

½ cup sour cream, room temperature

½ cup chopped chives

2 teaspoons ground pepper

DIRECTIONS

1. Place the potatoes in a large saucepan and cover with water. Season with salt. Bring to a boil over high heat and cook until the potatoes are very tender, 25 to 30 minutes. Drain.

2. While the potatoes cook, melt the butter in a skillet over medium heat. Add the garlic and cook until just fragrant, about 30 seconds. Remove from the heat and set aside.

3. Return the potatoes to the saucepan and add the garlic butter, milk, and sour cream. Mash together using a potato masher. Alternatively, use a potato ricer, then combine the riced potatoes with the garlic butter, milk, and sour cream. Stir in the chives, salt, and pepper. Serve immediately.

Sour Cream Potato Salad

Serves 4 to 6

Potato salad is ubiquitous at potlucks and barbecues, and this version is rich and creamy without feeling quite as heavy as some mayo-laden recipes. Sour cream is a natural topping for baked potatoes, so why not use it in potato salad? The flavors in this salad blend beautifully, so you can make it up to two days ahead of time with good results. This recipe was inspired by Molly Baz's Sour Cream and Onion Potato Salad in *Bon Appétit*.

2½ pounds Yukon Gold or fingerling potatoes, cut into 1-inch pieces

1 teaspoon kosher salt, plus more for cooking water

½ cup sliced red onion or shallot, plus more for garnish

1 cup sour cream

¼ cup mayonnaise

2 tablespoons capers

1 tablespoon Dijon mustard

1 teaspoon onion powder

½ teaspoon garlic powder

½ teaspoon ground pepper

¼ cup chopped dill, plus more for garnish

DIRECTIONS

1. Place the potatoes in a Dutch oven or large pot. Cover with cold water and season generously with salt. Bring to a boil over high heat, then cover and cook until the potatoes are tender, 10 to 15 minutes. Drain and set aside.

2. Rinse the onions with cold water and set aside. Place the sour cream, mayonnaise, capers, mustard, onion powder, garlic powder, salt, and pepper in a large serving bowl. Whisk to combine.

3. Add the potatoes and stir to coat. If desired, cover and refrigerate for up to 2 days.

4. Before serving, sprinkle the potatoes with red onion and dill.

CHICKEN, MEAT & SEAFOOD

You won't find recipes for pot roast in this cookbook—or meat loaf, or very much red meat at all.

That's mostly because of how we eat on a daily basis, but it was also true of my family when I was growing up—my dad is a hunter, and if we were eating meat, we were much more likely to have venison than beef. We're not vegetarians, but eating less beef is one way to lessen the impact of our diet on the planet.

Of course, this being a Minnesota cookbook, I had to include Juicy Lucy's (page 146), the Twin Cities' burger claim to fame. If you don't have a trip planned to Matt's Bar in Minneapolis or The Nook in St. Paul (both allege that they invented the molten cheese-stuffed burger), don't worry. This burger is easy to replicate at home and makes for an ideal summer dinner al fresco.

Fresh fish abounds in the Midwest all summer long, especially walleye, perch, trout, and other lake fish. If you have access to a lake and a fishing pole, so much the better. Although walleye is hard to find outside of the Midwest and Canada, it is worth seeking out if you can find it for the Fried Walleye Sandwiches (page 132), a take on classic fried fish dinners popular in Wisconsin year-round—a tradition stemming from the many Catholic immigrants to the area who abstained from eating meat on Fridays. Aquavit Moules Frites (page 129) may seem like a bit of an anomaly in a book focusing primarily on Midwestern and Scandinavian foods, but this ended up being one of my favorite recipes to work on—and adding aquavit, the Scandinavian liqueur, brings new flavors to the classic French preparation.

Chicken, of course, is a staple on American dinner tables across the country, and the Midwest is no exception. I'm always looking for new ways to spice up poultry, and Caraway Roast Chicken (page 125) might just be my new preferred method. Coated in a blend of spices, and roasted with fennel and onions until tender and caramelized, you won't be able to resist mopping up all the juices with plenty of crusty bread. Cornflake-Crusted Chicken (page 128) is my version of chicken tenders, an easy weeknight meal sure to please both adults and kids alike, while one-pan Chicken & Potato Skillet (page 126) is a flavorful yet easy method to prepare tender chicken thighs and crispy potatoes without much fuss.

Caraway Roast Chicken

Serves 4 to 6

Caraway is often found in Northern European cooking, most commonly in rye bread and sauerkraut, but the mild, anise-flavored herb is used in a number of Indian and Middle Eastern dishes as well. This mellow roast chicken pairs well with a variety of side dishes, including Scalloped Potatoes (page 117), Cabbage Salad with Caraway Seeds (page 56), and Apple & Fennel Salad (page 63). Don't forget some crusty bread to soak up all the delicious pan juices!

One 3½- to 4-pound chicken

2 tablespoons kosher salt

1 tablespoon ground pepper

1 tablespoon caraway seeds

2 teaspoons fennel seeds

1 teaspoon coriander seeds

¼ cup (½ stick) unsalted butter, melted

2 garlic cloves, minced

1 tablespoon chopped fresh thyme, plus more for garnish

1 lemon, cut into quarters

1 yellow onion, peeled and cut into quarters (leave the root end attached)

1 fennel bulb, trimmed and cut into quarters

DIRECTIONS

1. Preheat oven to 425°F. Pat the chicken dry with paper towels. Season all over with the salt and pepper. Let it sit at room temperature while you prepare the spice mix.

2. Heat the caraway, fennel, and coriander seeds in a dry skillet over medium heat. Toast until the spices begin to brown and smell fragrant, 1 to 2 minutes. Transfer to a spice grinder or mortar and pestle. Coarsely grind. Transfer spices to a small bowl.

3. Add the butter, garlic, and thyme to the bowl with spices. Stir together to form a paste.

4. Generously brush the butter mixture all over the chicken. Place the chicken breast side up in a 9-by-13-inch roasting pan. Tuck the wings under the chicken. Place a lemon quarter inside the cavity and tie the legs together with kitchen twine (if desired).

5. Scatter the onion, fennel bulb, and remaining lemons around the chicken. Roast until the skin begins to brown, about 40 minutes.

6. Reduce oven temperature to 375°F. Stir the onions, fennel, and lemons in the pan. Roast until the chicken is golden brown and the internal temperature reads 160°F on an instant-read thermometer when inserted into the thickest part of the thigh, 35 to 45 minutes more. Let rest for 10 minutes before carving. Carve into pieces. Serve with the lemon, onion, fennel, and additional fresh thyme.

Chicken & Potato Skillet

Serves 4

This easy, one-pan dinner was inspired by Melissa Clark's delicious Sheet-Pan Chicken with Potatoes, Arugula, and Garlic Yogurt from the *New York Times*, and it's perfect for busy weeknights and cool fall evenings. Fingerling potatoes have a particularly buttery flavor and texture, which pairs well with chicken. Serve with a simple Butter Lettuce Salad with Creamy Mustard Dressing (page 52) or fresh arugula. The yogurt sauce is optional, but I like the creamy, tangy element it adds to the chicken—alternatively, try it with your favorite hot sauce and crusty bread.

CHICKEN & POTATOES

3 tablespoons olive oil

2 garlic cloves, minced

2 teaspoons smoked paprika

2 teaspoons kosher salt

1 teaspoon ground pepper

4 skin-on, bone-in chicken thighs

2 pounds fingerling or small waxy potatoes, cut in half

2 small shallots, thinly sliced

Chopped dill or parsley for garnish

YOGURT SAUCE

1 cup Greek yogurt

2 tablespoons chopped dill or parsley

1 tablespoon lemon zest

1 tablespoon lemon juice

½ teaspoon kosher salt

DIRECTIONS

1. Whisk the olive oil, garlic, paprika, 2 teaspoons salt, and pepper together in a large bowl. Add the chicken, potatoes, and shallots to the bowl and stir well to coat. Let sit at room temperature for 30 minutes, or refrigerate for up to 6 hours.

2. Preheat oven to 350°F.

3. Place the chicken skin side down in a cold ovenproof skillet. Turn the heat to medium-high. Cook until very browned and the thighs don't stick to the pan, 5 to 7 minutes. Move the chicken pieces around a little and cook 2 to 3 minutes more, until evenly browned.

4. Remove the chicken to a plate. Add the potatoes and shallots to the skillet and stir in the pan drippings. (Careful, they might splatter!) Return the chicken to the pan, nestling it over the potatoes.

5. Bake the chicken and potatoes for 35 to 45 minutes, until the chicken and potatoes are well browned and tender and an instant-read thermometer reads 165°F when inserted into the thickest part of the chicken thighs. Stir the potatoes halfway through the cooking time.

6. **MAKE THE YOGURT SAUCE:** While the chicken bakes, mix the yogurt, dill, lemon zest and juice, and ½ teaspoon salt in a small bowl.

7. Sprinkle the dill over the chicken and serve with the yogurt sauce.

Cornflake-Crusted Chicken

Serves 4 to 6

Think of this easy chicken dish as an alternative to fried chicken tenders (though I'm a big fan of those, too). The meat becomes super tender thanks to the buttermilk brine, and crushed cornflakes make for a crispy exterior with plenty of crunch. Be sure to crush the cornflakes finely, as they will adhere better to the chicken. This is a great kid-friendly dinner when served with a hearty salad and roasted potatoes.

2 cups buttermilk

2 tablespoons plus ½ teaspoon kosher salt

2 teaspoons onion powder

2 teaspoons garlic powder

1 teaspoon ground pepper

2 pounds chicken breasts, cut into 1- to 2-inch strips

2 cups cornflakes

2 tablespoons olive oil

Dipping sauces for serving

DIRECTIONS

1. Whisk the buttermilk, 2 tablespoons of the salt, onion powder, garlic powder, and pepper together in a large bowl or resealable plastic bag. Add the chicken pieces to the mixture, cover or seal, and refrigerate for at least 2 hours or up to 24.

2. When ready to bake, preheat oven to 400°F. Line two rimmed baking sheets with parchment paper.

3. Place the cornflakes and ½ teaspoon of the salt in the body of a food processor or large resealable plastic bag. Process or crush into fine crumbs. Transfer to a large plate.

4. Remove the chicken from the brine and place on a large plate. Coat each chicken piece in cornflake crumbs, pressing to adhere. Place the chicken pieces on the prepared baking sheets.

5. Heat the oil in a large skillet over medium-high heat. Working in batches, cook the chicken pieces until browned, about 3 minutes per side. Return to the baking sheet and repeat with the remaining chicken.

6. Bake the chicken for 20 to 25 minutes, until crispy and cooked through.

Aquavit Moules Frites

Serves 4 to 6

I worked at the wonderful French restaurant Meritage in St. Paul after college, and their incredible mussels in white wine sauce with pommes frites remains one of my favorite dishes of all time. Inspired by the classic Francophone pairing, this recipe uses Scandinavian flavors like aquavit in addition to garlic and cream. You can skip the fries if you like and serve the mussels with crusty bread instead (or in addition to)—but they are best enjoyed on a warm summer night with a glass of crisp white wine. For the true Meritage experience at home, serve the mussels and fries with a decadent béarnaise sauce.

BÉARNAISE

½ cup butter (1 stick)

3 tablespoons chopped shallots

1 tablespoon plus 1 teaspoon white wine vinegar

2 egg yolks

2 teaspoons lemon juice

¼ teaspoon kosher salt, plus more if needed

2 teaspoons chopped parsley, tarragon, or marjoram

POMMES FRITES

6 russet potatoes

½ teaspoon kosher salt, plus more for seasoning

Vegetable or peanut oil for frying

Flaky sea salt, such as Maldon

AQUAVIT MOULES

3 tablespoons butter

2 shallots, finely chopped

2 garlic cloves, finely chopped

1 fennel bulb, trimmed and thinly sliced (reserve the fronds for garnish if desired)

½ cup aquavit

¼ cup dry vermouth or white wine

½ cup heavy cream

1 teaspoon kosher salt

½ teaspoon ground pepper

½ teaspoon fennel seeds

2 pounds black mussels, scrubbed and debearded

½ cup chopped parsley, tarragon, or marjoram, or a mix

Crusty bread for serving

CONTINUED ▶

DIRECTIONS

1. **MAKE THE BÉARNAISE:** Fill your blender with warm water (this will help keep the sauce stable).

2. Melt 1 tablespoon of the butter in a skillet over medium heat. Add the shallots and cook until beginning to brown, about 3 minutes. Add the vinegar and cook until liquid has nearly evaporated, about 2 minutes. Set aside and cool completely.

3. Pour out the water from the blender and dry completely. Melt the remaining 7 tablespoons butter in a small saucepan over medium heat. Transfer to a glass measuring cup.

4. Place the egg yolks, lemon juice, and salt in the blender. Blend until combined, about 10 seconds. With the blender running, slowly add the butter drop by drop, until the sauce is thick and emulsified. Discard any milk solids in the measuring cup.

5. Transfer the sauce to a small bowl. Stir in the shallot reduction and chopped herbs. Season with salt if necessary. Cover tightly with plastic wrap and keep at room temperature for up to 1 hour.

6. **MAKE THE POMMES FRITES:** Cut the potatoes into ¼-inch-thick slices. Cut again into ¼- to ½-inch-thick matchsticks.

7. Place the potatoes and salt in a large bowl of ice water. Soak for 30 minutes. Drain and thoroughly dry with a dishcloth or paper towels.

8. Place a rack over a rimmed baking sheet. Fill a large saucepan or Dutch oven 3 inches high with peanut or vegetable oil. Heat to 325°F over medium-high. Working in batches, fry the potatoes until beginning to brown, 3 to 5 minutes. Remove to the prepared rack. Repeat with the remaining potatoes. This can be done up to 3 hours ahead.

9. Just before serving, heat the oil to 375°F. Working in batches, fry the potatoes again until golden brown and crispy, about 1 minute. Remove to a paper towel–lined plate and sprinkle with the sea salt. Repeat with the remaining fries. Serve immediately.

10. **PREPARE THE MUSSELS:** Melt the butter in a Dutch oven or stockpot over medium heat. Add the shallots, garlic, and fennel and cook until softened, about 5 minutes. Add the aquavit and vermouth and cook for 1 to 2 minutes to burn off some of the alcohol. Add the cream, salt, pepper, and fennel seeds and stir to combine. Add the mussels, then cover the pot and cook until the mussels have opened, about 5 minutes. Discard any mussels that have not opened. Sprinkle with fresh herbs and fennel fronds, if using, and serve immediately with crusty bread, pommes frites, and béarnaise.

Fried Walleye Sandwiches

Serves 6

There's something about fried fish sandwiches that screams summer to me, and this one just cries out to be consumed on a warm afternoon with an ice cold lager (of course, that doesn't mean it's not still delicious on a cool fall evening as well). Walleye is a large freshwater fish, and it's widely available in the Midwest and Canada, but you can use whatever firm white fish is freshest at your local market, such as cod, sea bass, or halibut.

TARTAR SAUCE

½ cup mayonnaise

¼ cup chopped Refrigerator Pickles (page 113), bread and butter pickles, or relish

Zest and juice of 1 small lemon

1 tablespoon Dijon mustard

1 tablespoon chopped capers

1 tablespoon chopped chives

Kosher salt

Ground pepper

SANDWICHES

2 pounds walleye fillets, cut into 6 pieces

1½ cups all-purpose flour

2 teaspoons Old Bay seasoning

1½ teaspoons baking powder

1 teaspoon kosher salt, plus more for seasoning

½ teaspoon cayenne (optional)

Canola or vegetable oil for frying

1½ cups lager

4 toasted hot dog buns for serving

Refrigerator Pickles (page 113) or bread and butter pickles for serving

Chopped iceberg lettuce for serving

Note

Walleye fillets are very thin. If using a thicker cut of fish, add 1 to 2 minutes to the cooking time.

DIRECTIONS

1. **MAKE THE TARTAR SAUCE:** Mix the mayonnaise, pickles, lemon zest and juice, mustard, capers, and chives in a small bowl. Season to taste with salt and pepper. Refrigerate until ready to use.

2. **MAKE THE SANDWICHES:** Pat the fish dry with paper towels. Whisk the flour, Old Bay, baking powder, salt, and cayenne together in a large bowl.

3. Add 2 inches oil to a cast-iron skillet or Dutch oven. Place over medium heat until the oil reaches 375°F.

4. Just before the oil reaches the 375°F temperature, add the beer to the flour mixture. Whisk until just combined (it will be lumpy). Add 2 fillets to the batter and flip to coat.

5. Add the battered fillets to the oil and fry until golden brown on both sides, about 3 minutes. Monitor the oil temperature as you cook; it will likely drop when you add fish. Use tongs to transfer the fish to a paper towel–lined plate or wire rack and season with salt. Repeat with the remaining fillets.

6. To serve, spread each bun with tartar sauce and layer with pickles, fried fish, and lettuce. Serve immediately.

Slow-Roasted Trout with Citrus & Fennel

Serves 4 to 6

Whole fish can feel intimidating, but it's actually even easier than roasting a chicken! Your fishmonger will do all the hard work for you by removing the organs and large bones, and it makes for an impressive presentation while hardly taking any work on your part. In Minnesota, lake trout is popular during the summer fishing season, but whatever trout or whole fish you can find will do. Slow roasting the fish at a lower temperature followed by a quick steam in the pan results in tender, buttery fish, delicately flavored with citrus, fennel, and fresh herbs. It's sure to be a year-round dinner party hit.

2 tablespoons olive oil, plus more for drizzling

One 3½-pound whole steelhead or lake trout, or 4 whole rainbow trout (about ¾ pound each, see Note)

2 tablespoons kosher salt, plus more for seasoning

1 fennel bulb, very thinly sliced

1 orange, thinly sliced

1 lemon, thinly sliced

1 small red onion or shallot, thinly sliced

2 garlic cloves, thinly sliced

2 tablespoons capers, drained

Fresh dill or parsley

DIRECTIONS

1. Preheat oven to 300°F. Line a rimmed baking sheet with aluminum foil or parchment paper and coat with 2 tablespoons olive oil.

2. Rub the skin of the fish generously with 2 tablespoons salt to remove the slimy coating. Leave on the salt for a few minutes, then rinse with cold water. Pat very dry with paper towels.

3. Place the trout on the prepared baking sheet and season all over (inside and outside) with salt. Layer some of the fennel, orange, lemon, red onion slices, and garlic inside the trout. Scatter the remaining fennel, citrus, onions, and dill around the fish on the baking sheet. Sprinkle with capers and drizzle generously with more olive oil. Cover the pan tightly with aluminum foil.

4. Roast the trout for 25 minutes. Turn off the oven and let the trout sit in the hot oven for another 15 to 20 minutes, until very tender and buttery.

5. If serving one large whole fish, use a fork and spoon to delicately lift the flesh from the skin and distribute the citrus and vegetables among guests. If serving smaller whole fish, serve one to each guest.

Note

This preparation works for any type of delicate, whole fish—if you can't get trout, try with branzino or sea bass, or whatever is freshest at your local fish market. You can also layer the citrus and fennel on top of a large (3 to 4 pounds) fillet of delicate white fish, such as halibut or monkfish.

Braised Roast Beef Sandwiches

Serves 8

These tender beef sandwiches are loosely inspired by the crockpot roast beef sandwiches my dad's cousin Lorraine used to serve at her annual Memorial Day gathering when I was little. I'm pretty sure she used Lipton Onion Soup Mix packets as seasoning (nothing wrong with that!), and there was always enough for the numerous distant relatives who would drive in from all over Minnesota to eat, drink, and celebrate the beginning of summer. In this version, tender short ribs and chuck roast are slowly braised in the oven, then served with their own au jus as a dipping sauce, a little like birria tacos or French dip sandwiches. The horseradish cream is optional, but highly recommended!

ROAST BEEF SANDWICHES

3 pounds chuck roast, cut into large chunks

1½ pounds bone-in short ribs

2 tablespoons kosher salt, plus more for seasoning

1 tablespoon olive oil

1 small yellow onion, chopped

2 garlic cloves, chopped

2 cups beef broth

2 cups water

¼ cup apple cider vinegar

¼ cup ketchup

2 tablespoons brown sugar

2 tablespoons Worcestershire sauce

1 tablespoon ground mustard

1 canned chipotle chile in adobo sauce

Ground pepper

8 toasted ciabatta rolls for serving

Choice of mustard and pickles
   for serving (optional)

Arugula for serving

HORSERADISH CREAM

¼ cup heavy whipping cream

½ cup sour cream or crème fraîche

⅓ cup jarred or fresh horseradish

2 tablespoons minced chives

1 tablespoon lemon juice

Kosher salt

Ground pepper

DIRECTIONS

1. **MAKE THE ROAST BEEF:** Season the chuck roast and short ribs all over with 2 tablespoons salt. Preheat oven to 300°F.

2. Heat the olive oil in a large Dutch oven or ovenproof skillet over medium-high heat. Working in batches if needed, sear the chuck roast pieces and short ribs until deeply browned on all sides, about 10 minutes per batch. Remove to a plate and repeat until all the pieces of beef are browned. Add the onion to the pan and cook until beginning to soften and brown, 5 to 8 minutes. Add the garlic and cook for 1 minute.

3. Add the broth, water, vinegar, ketchup, brown sugar, Worcestershire sauce, mustard, and chipotle chile to the pot and bring to a simmer. Return the beef to the pot and remove from the heat. Season well with salt and pepper.

4. Cover and transfer to the oven. Bake until very tender and falling off the bone, stirring occasionally if needed, about 4 hours.

CONTINUED ▶

5. **MAKE THE HORSERADISH CREAM:** While the beef cooks, place the whipping cream in a medium bowl and whisk just until soft peaks form. Fold in the sour cream, horseradish, chives, and lemon juice. Season with salt and pepper. Refrigerate until ready to use.

6. Remove the beef to a bowl and shred the meat, leaving the cooking liquid in the pot. Discard the bones and any excess fat. Season with salt and pepper if needed. Cover with foil to keep warm.

7. Bring the cooking liquid to a boil over medium-high heat. Reduce the heat to medium-low and simmer for about 30 minutes, until the sauce has reduced by half. Transfer to a small serving bowl.

8. Serve the beef on toasted ciabatta rolls with horseradish cream, au jus, mustard, pickles, and/or arugula, if desired.

Swedish Meatballs

Makes 20 to 25

There's no other dish that so immediately tastes like "home" to me than tender Swedish meatballs. My family eats these annually on Christmas Eve, and it has always been a meal we look forward to all year long. Though many more people are now familiar with the dish thanks to Ikea, making your own at home is worth the time and effort. The meatballs are super tender thanks to the soaked bread in the mixture, and don't skimp on browning them well in the pan—all those tasty bits help flavor the creamy gravy.

In my family we always enjoy these with mashed potatoes, sautéed green beans, lutefisk, lefse, and Jell-O salad on the side—the mashed potatoes are mandatory, but many Midwesterners also serve them with lingonberry jam. These meatballs would also be quite tasty on a sandwich, similar to an Italian meatball sub.

MEATBALLS

½ cup milk

1 cup cubed French or white bread

1½ pounds ground beef

1 pound ground pork

1 egg

1 yellow onion, chopped

2 tablespoons instant oatmeal

2 teaspoons kosher salt

½ teaspoon ground pepper

¼ teaspoon allspice

¼ teaspoon ground cloves

¼ cup butter, or as needed

GRAVY

¼ cup butter

¼ cup flour

2 cups chicken or beef broth, warmed

1 cup whole milk, warmed

½ teaspoon kosher salt

½ teaspoon ground pepper

Chopped parsley for garnish

DIRECTIONS

1. Preheat oven to 325°F. Line a rimmed baking sheet with parchment paper. In a small bowl, pour the milk over the bread and let soak for 10 minutes.

2. Mix the beef, pork, egg, ½ cup of the chopped onion, oatmeal, salt, pepper, allspice, and cloves in a large bowl. Use your hands to break up the bread, and add the bread-milk mixture to the meat. Use your hands to combine until fully mixed.

3. Shape the mixture into 2-inch balls and place on the prepared baking sheet.

4. Melt 1 tablespoon of the butter in a large skillet over medium-high heat. Add the remaining onion to the pan and stir to coat with butter, then push to one side of skillet. Working in batches, add a few meatballs at a time and brown on all sides, about 5 minutes. Return the cooked meatballs to the baking sheet and repeat with the remaining meatballs. Stir the onion between batches of meatballs. Add more butter to the pan as needed.

CONTINUED ▶

5. When all the meatballs are browned, leave the onions in the pan (they will be browned and caramelized by now). Bake the meatballs for 20 to 25 minutes, until cooked through.

6. **MAKE THE GRAVY:** Melt butter in the skillet with the onions over medium heat, scraping up any drippings. Add the flour and cook until browned and nutty, whisking constantly, about 3 minutes.

7. Add the chicken broth ½ cup at a time, whisking thoroughly after each addition. Repeat with the milk. Cook the gravy over medium-low heat until thickened, about 5 minutes. Season with salt and pepper.

8. To serve, spoon the gravy over the meatballs and garnish with parsley.

On Scandinavian Ingredients

When I was growing up, my parents, sisters, and I gathered with my cousins at my grandma Veola's house in Lakeville, Minnesota, at least once a month. It was typical for the meal to begin with an appetizer spread of herring, pickles, and saltines, and perhaps some cream cheese with red pepper jelly. On Christmas Eve, in addition to our usual Swedish meatballs, there is always lutefisk: dried cod pickled in lye and rehydrated to form a somewhat gelatinous fish doused in melted butter. In fact, across Minnesota and Wisconsin traditional lutefisk dinners are popular gatherings in church basements in the days leading up to Christmas.

While salt cod remains one of Scandinavia's main exports, and is popular across Europe, lutefisk is rarely consumed these days in Norway and Sweden. But it's a tradition that has lived on for generations in the upper Midwest, preserved by the descendants of immigrants who came here in the late nineteenth and early twentieth centuries. Despite its gelatinous texture and fishy taste, lutefisk remains a stalwart of Scandinavian heritage in Minnesota, including in my own family, as a way to hold on to the traditions of these ancestors. The exact origin of lutefisk is unclear, but legend has it the dish dates back to the Vikings. It was created to preserve fish through the long, dark winters, and references to it are found in Norwegian literature as early as the mid-sixteenth century.

A number of other exports from Norway and Sweden live on across the upper Midwest, some of which have become more familiar around the country thanks to Ikea. Who can argue with the appeal of gravy-covered Swedish meatballs and tart lingonberry jam? Other items like gjetost (Norwegian brown cheese made from whey) and dried salt cod may not be available at local grocery stores in Nevada or South Carolina, but they are widely available online. The same goes for other foods like lefse, gravlax, and dense rye crackers.

While you won't find a recipe for lutefisk in this book (and I can't say that I eat it on Christmas Eve, though my dad insists that sriracha improves the taste), I appreciate the adherence to tradition that these dishes maintain. I've never visited Norway, but preserving these food traditions is a way to maintain a connection with my great-great-great grandparents who came to Minnesota in search of a better life. They were humble, hardworking people, Lutheran farmers and fishermen who traveled for weeks in steamships across the Atlantic, seeking escape from the poverty and agricultural famines in Europe in the late 1800s. The vast majority of Norwegian and Swedish immigrants during this time period settled in rural areas across Minnesota, Wisconsin, and the Dakotas, and the cultural ties here are still strong today. Heritage organizations such as Sons of Norway and the American Swedish Institute in Minneapolis maintain an active membership, though their traditions and practices may have more in common with historic Norway, Sweden, and Denmark than these societies of the modern era. Our ties to the old country were born out of a nostalgia for the hardships our ancestors went through, as well as a desire to keep our connections to the family our ancestors left behind. Our ancestry is something to be proud of, preserved through holiday celebrations, traditional dress, and most directly, through food.

"... by preserving these food traditions, it's a way to maintain that connection with my great-great-great grandparents who came to Minnesota in search of a better life."

As the United States, including the upper Midwest, becomes more racially and culturally diverse, our country improves and expands in richness in cultural heritage and food traditions. We can maintain these ties to old European cultures while also welcoming new ones from across the globe. Indeed, my son Dashiell is a combination of my white Scandinavian heritage and his father's Northern California upbringing, his grandpa a Black bull rider from Oklahoma and his nanna the descendant of Lithuanian Jews who settled in Boston. He will grow up with brisket and latkes, carnitas tacos, and trips to In-N-Out Burger on visits to the Bay Area, as well as gravlax on rye crackers and afternoons spent rolling krumkake (a type of Scandinavian cookie) with my parents during the holidays. He may not be required to try a bite of lutefisk on Christmas Eve, as my sisters and I were (though the jury's still out on that one), but he will know both about his grandpa Jim's love of chitlins and his grandpa Randy's fondness for pickled herring. We celebrate with ham on Easter and apple cake on Rosh Hashanah, with smørrebrød in a smorgasbord brunch on Christmas Eve and fried chicken and waffles on his dad's birthday in February.

He may grow up in Minnesota, but his heritage is a true mixture of America: His great-great-great grandparents are Norwegian and Swedish farmers, Eastern European Jews, and freed enslaved people from Texas and Louisiana. We will teach him about Valdres, Norway, where his Ellingboe ancestors came from, but also about Boley, Oklahoma, one of several all-Black towns in the South, where the King family settled during Reconstruction. He will know lingonberry jam and lutefisk, as well as matzo ball soup during Passover. By maintaining our connections with these foods, we will show him where he came from, and who he can be.

Juicy Lucy's

Serves 6

The origins of the Juicy Lucy are debatable, although two dives, Matt's Bar in Minneapolis and The Nook in St. Paul, claim the honor. Luckily these burgers are easy to make at home—I like grilling on a cast-iron griddle on a warm summer night, but you can also cook on a griddle or skillet on your stove. American cheese is traditional for maximum meltability, though I prefer the flavor of sharp cheddar and that's what I use here. I have also made these with ground beef substitutes with good results. Serve with Pommes Frites (page 129), Sour Cream Potato Salad (page 119), or potato chips for an unbeatable summertime dinner.

BURGERS

1½ pounds ground beef

Kosher salt

Ground pepper

6 slices sharp cheddar cheese

2 tablespoons vegetable or canola oil

SECRET SAUCE

½ cup mayonnaise

½ cup chopped Refrigerator Pickles
   (page 113) or bread and butter pickles

¼ cup ketchup

1 teaspoon sriracha or other chile sauce

½ teaspoon kosher salt

TO SERVE

Potato rolls or burger buns of your choice

Butter lettuce

Sliced tomato

Sliced red onions

Refrigerator Pickles (page 113)
   or bread and butter pickles

DIRECTIONS

1. **MAKE THE BURGERS:** Shape the ground beef into 12 patties and flatten each one with your hand. Place 6 patties on a baking sheet. Season with salt and pepper. Place 1 slice of cheese on each patty, cutting the cheese in half or quarters if needed. Cover with the remaining 6 patties. Use your fingers to pinch the patties around the cheese to form a seal. Make sure it's secure, or the cheese will melt onto the griddle while cooking!

2. **MAKE THE SECRET SAUCE:** Mix the mayonnaise, pickles, ketchup, sriracha, and salt together in a small bowl.

3. Preheat a griddle or large cast-iron skillet on the grill over high heat for 20 minutes, until very hot. Water should sizzle if you sprinkle a few drops on top. Alternatively, preheat the griddle or skillet on the stove until smoking hot, about 10 minutes.

4. Heat the oil on the griddle until it begins to smoke. Depending on the size of your cooking surface, place 3 to 6 burgers on the griddle and cook until the edges are browned and beginning to crisp, about 3 minutes. Flip and cook until the burgers are cooked nearly through and browned on both sides, 2 to 3 minutes more. Repeat with the remaining patties.

5. **TO SERVE:** Spread each bun with secret sauce. Place a Juicy Lucy on the bun, then top with lettuce, tomato, onion, and pickles as desired. Serve immediately.

Pork Chops with Apple Mostarda

Serves 4

When I developed this recipe, I knew I wanted to highlight the natural pairing of tender pork and crisp fall apples, and this apple mostarda is the perfect accompaniment to buttery, tender pork chops. The cooking time for the mostarda is a couple of hours, but you can make it well in advance of the pork chops. The mostarda will keep in the refrigerator for a few weeks, so save any extra for Apple Gjetost Grilled Cheese (page 31) or serve with a cheese and charcuterie plate.

APPLE MOSTARDA

2 pounds apples (about 4 large), such as Honeycrisp or Gala, peeled, cored, and diced

½ cup packed brown sugar

2 tablespoons mustard seeds

1 tablespoon chopped fresh thyme leaves

2 teaspoons lemon zest

1 teaspoon kosher salt

½ teaspoon ground pepper

½ cup apple cider vinegar

½ cup apple juice, cider, or water

PORK CHOPS

Four 6-ounce or two 10-ounce bone-in pork chops

Kosher salt

Ground pepper

1 tablespoon vegetable or canola oil

2 tablespoons unsalted butter

2 sprigs fresh thyme

1 tablespoon apple cider vinegar

DIRECTIONS

1. **MAKE THE APPLE MOSTARDA:** Combine the apples, brown sugar, mustard seeds, thyme, lemon zest, salt, and pepper in a large saucepan or Dutch oven. Bring to a boil over medium-high heat, then reduce heat to a simmer and cover. Stir in the vinegar and apple juice. Cook, stirring occasionally, until the mostarda becomes thick and jammy, 1½ to 2 hours.

2. **MAKE THE PORK CHOPS:** Preheat oven to 400°F. Season the pork chops generously with salt and pepper on both sides.

3. Heat the oil in a heavy ovenproof skillet over medium-high heat until smoking. Add the pork chops. Sear each side until well browned and the fat is beginning to crisp, 1 to 2 minutes per side. Add the butter and thyme to the pan and remove from the heat. Spoon the butter over the pork chops.

4. Transfer the pan to the oven and bake until an instant-read thermometer registers 140°F when inserted into the thickest part of the chop, 6 to 10 minutes. Remove the pan from the oven and add the vinegar to the pan juices. Let rest for 10 minutes, then cut the pork into slices. Spoon the pan juices over the slices and serve with the apple mostarda.

Sweet Potato & Sausage Skillet

Serves 4

I always picture eating this one-pan dish while wrapped in a plaid wool blanket at a tailgate party, accompanied by a warm cup of spiked apple cider. This skillet dish makes a perfect fall dinner, and would be easy to cook over an open fire or grill for alfresco meals on cool evenings. If you're like us, serve with plenty of hot sauce.

1 pound Italian sausage links (sweet or spicy)

1 cup water

2 tablespoons olive oil

2 pounds sweet potatoes, cut into ½-inch pieces (see Note)

½ cup sliced yellow onion

1 apple, cored and cut into ½-inch pieces

1 teaspoon caraway seeds

1 teaspoon kosher salt

½ teaspoon ground pepper

2 tablespoons chopped parsley

1 tablespoon chopped chives

DIRECTIONS

1. Heat a large skillet over medium-high heat. Add the sausage and water and cook, turning the sausage occasionally, until the water has evaporated, about 10 minutes. Brown the sausages on all sides until cooked through, 5 to 8 minutes more. Remove from the skillet and set aside. Slice into coins if desired.

2. Heat the oil in the skillet over medium heat. Add the sweet potatoes, onion, apple, and caraway seeds and stir to coat. Season with the salt and pepper. Cover and cook for 15 minutes, stirring occasionally.

3. Return the sausage to the skillet and stir into the vegetables. Cook for another 5 minutes, stirring occasionally, until the sausages are heated through and the potatoes are tender. Sprinkle with parsley and chives, and serve immediately.

Note

I often don't peel sweet potatoes as the skins contain lots of good nutrients, but be sure to give them a good scrub! Feel free to peel them if you prefer.

Venison Tenderloin with Lingonberry-Red Wine Sauce

Serves 6

We ate venison more often than beef when I was growing up. Given the popularity of hunting in the Midwest, it's common for families to have a stash of venison in their freezer. (Choosing venison over beef is also better for the planet!) If prepared well, venison has a complex taste that's not at all gamey, and it pairs nicely with tannic lingonberries and red wine.

Be sure not to overcook the venison—as with high-quality steak, it should be cooked to medium-rare for best results. I like searing in a cast-iron skillet for the most control, but the tenderloins can also be grilled over high heat.

VENISON TENDERLOIN

½ cup olive oil

Zest and juice of 1 lemon

2 tablespoons roughly chopped rosemary

2 garlic cloves, smashed

1 tablespoon kosher salt

2 teaspoons ground pepper

1 teaspoon dried juniper berries, crushed

2 pounds venison tenderloin or steaks

1 tablespoon canola or grapeseed oil

LINGONBERRY-RED WINE SAUCE

¾ cup dry red wine

¾ cup venison or beef stock

¼ cup lingonberry preserves

1 teaspoon juniper berries, crushed

¼ teaspoon ground pepper

2 tablespoons butter

Fresh rosemary for garnish

DIRECTIONS

1. **MAKE THE TENDERLOIN:** Combine the olive oil, lemon zest and juice, rosemary, garlic, salt, pepper, and juniper berries in a shallow baking dish or resealable plastic bag. Add the venison and coat with the marinade to cover. Marinate for at least 4 hours or overnight.

2. **MAKE THE LINGONBERRY-RED WINE SAUCE:** Bring the wine and stock to a simmer in a saucepan over medium heat. Cook until reduced by half, about 20 minutes. Stir in the preserves, juniper berries, and pepper and cook for 5 minutes more. Remove from the heat.

3. When ready to cook, preheat a cast-iron skillet or griddle over high heat until smoking. Remove the venison from the marinade and pat dry. Add the canola oil to the pan, then add the venison. Sear, flipping once, until the surface is well browned and the meat is medium-rare, about 5 minutes total. Let rest for 10 minutes before serving.

4. Just before serving, heat the sauce over medium-low heat and stir in the butter until melted. Cut the venison into slices and serve with the lingonberry-red wine sauce and fresh rosemary.

GATHERINGS

There's nothing I love more than a dinner party.

I love planning elaborate menus, starting preparations days ahead of time, and setting the table with clean linens and fresh flowers. The anticipation of enjoying a quiet glass of wine while finishing last-minute preparations before the first guest arrives—there's nothing like it. And once family and friends walk through the door, there's nothing more satisfying than a well-executed gathering, one where the drinks never stop flowing, the food is abundant, and conversation flows easily and naturally. I don't even mind the cleanup, knowing that everyone enjoyed themselves and it was a night well spent.

My family has a long history of large gatherings: My parents regularly host anywhere from 30 to 60 people for Thanksgiving dinner, and our 165-person wedding was held at their house. When I was growing up, they hosted barn dances every fall, complete with square dancing and hot apple cider. I started planning dinner parties in high school, and they are one of my favorite things to this day. Come summer, you'll find me spreading newspaper across the table on our deck, a pot of crayfish, potatoes, and sweet corn boiling on the stove, rosé and beer on ice, awaiting our friends' arrival. For New Year's Eve, I'll create a spread of appetizers accompanied by chilled sparkling wine, culminating with decadent fondue as we approach midnight.

This chapter centers on gatherings: one for each season, anchored by food that's meant to be enjoyed by a group. Each takes some advance planning, but the effort is well worth it: imagine the gasps when you bring out a glistening Maple-Glazed Ham (page 189), or the feeling of cracking open crayfish and fresh corn on the cob for a midsummer Kräftskiva feast (page 180). While each of these menus is undeniably about the food (as it should be for any good dinner party), they are also designed to promote a feeling of togetherness and interaction. Each requires participation from your guests, from dipping bread and apples into Norwegian Fondue (page 164) to assembling their own open-face smørrebrød sandwiches with Gravlax (page 172), cream cheese, and hard-boiled eggs. And don't forget the cocktails—I don't think there's ever a party that can't benefit from a signature cocktail, and it's a perfect way to welcome your guests upon arrival. I'm particularly partial to the Aquavit Martini (page 160) for a bracing aperitif, but don't sleep on the Bootlegger Jell-O Shots (page 168)—they're a surprisingly delicious and citrusy upgrade from the ones you tried in college.

WINTER
Norwegian Fondue
Party Menu
159

SPRING
Smorgasbord
Brunch Menu
167

SUMMER
Midsummer
Kräftskiva Menu
177

FALL
Maple-Glazed Ham
Buffet Menu
185

WINTER

Norwegian Fondue
Party Menu

Aquavit Martini 160

Glögg 163

Norwegian Fondue 164

Butter Lettuce Salad with Creamy
Mustard Dressing 52

Apple Crisp 201

Vanilla Ice Cream 227

Aquavit Martini

Makes 1

Aquavit is a spirit that's ubiquitous across Scandinavia, but it's just beginning to catch on in the United States. It's long been popular in Minnesota—often served as a bracing shot to ward off the winter cold. But its unique herbal flavors lend themselves well to cocktails, too. There are several different varieties, from Norwegian oak barrel–aged Linie to citrusy Swedish Ahus, and in Minnesota we're now lucky to have a number of local distilleries producing the spirit. Some of my favorites include Tattersall, Vikre, and Norseman.

Because I was pregnant while writing this book, my sister Solveig helped me test all the cocktail recipes. She prefers an extra dry martini, but we both love the floral note that Lillet adds to this refreshing drink. If you're like her, start with ¼ ounce Lillet and add more if you desire.

2½ ounces aquavit
½ ounce Lillet blanc
Lemon twist

DIRECTIONS

1. Pour the aquavit and Lillet into a cocktail shaker and fill with ice. Shake until it's so cold you almost can't hold the shaker, about 30 seconds.

2. Strain into a chilled martini glass and garnish with a lemon twist.

Glögg

Serves 8 to 10

Though this mulled wine is a longstanding winter tradition in Norway and Sweden, it was a relatively recent discovery by my immediate family. When I was living in New York City in my early 20s and flew home for Christmas each year, my parents introduced a winter solstice celebration to make the most of the short week we were all together, which mainly consists of sitting around a bonfire with a warm mug of glögg.

As we moved our gatherings outside during the pandemic winter of 2020 to 2021, drinking glögg became the norm as I began writing this book. Whether sipped by a fire or in the comfort of your own home, this fortified, spiced wine is sure to warm you up on even the coldest days.

6 cardamom pods, crushed

4 whole cloves

2 star anise

2 cinnamon sticks, broken into pieces

1-inch piece of ginger, thinly sliced

Two 750-ml bottles dry red wine

1½ cups sugar

375 ml aquavit, vodka, or brandy

½ cup whole blanched almonds

½ cup golden raisins

Orange slices for garnish

DIRECTIONS

1. Place the cardamom, cloves, star anise, cinnamon, and ginger on a small square of cheesecloth or muslin. Use kitchen string to tie the edges of the cheesecloth together to form a small bag. Alternatively, add the spices directly into the pot with the wine—you will just need to remove them later when serving.

2. Place the wine in a Dutch oven or other large pot over medium-high heat. Add the spice bag and sugar and stir until the sugar is dissolved. Remove from the heat, cover, and cool for 2 hours or overnight.

3. When ready to serve, return the wine to the heat and add the aquavit. Heat until the mixture is just about to come to a boil. Stir in the almonds and raisins, and ladle into mugs garnished with an orange slice.

Norwegian Fondue

Serves 8 to 10

When I was little, my grandma Nancy, grandpa LeRoy, parents, aunts, and uncles would often make fondue to celebrate New Year's Eve. It's fallen out of fashion in recent years, but I think it's high time for a comeback. What's not to love about creamy melted cheese? It's also a perfect winter party food, since it comes together quickly and stays warm over a flame.

Jarlsberg is a mild cheese similar to Gruyère or Swiss. It's widely available, but if you can't find Jarlsberg, try one of those alternatives instead. Kirsch is traditionally added to fondue, but for a Scandinavian spin, I like a splash of aquavit. Serve with dry white wine, such as Sancerre or sauvignon blanc, or accompanied by Aquavit Martinis (page 160).

FONDUE

1 pound Jarlsberg cheese, grated

½ pound Havarti or Emmentaler cheese, grated

2 tablespoons cornstarch

1 garlic clove, cut in half

1½ cups dry white wine

1 tablespoon aquavit or vodka

Ground pepper

Pinch of ground nutmeg

SERVING SUGGESTIONS

Fresh bread, cut into small slices or cubes

Boiled new potatoes

Apple slices

Blanched green beans

Sliced hard salami

Cornichons

DIRECTIONS

1. Mix the Jarlsberg, Havarti, and cornstarch together in a large bowl until the cheese is lightly coated.

2. Heat a large saucepan over medium heat. Rub the garlic clove across the bottom of the pan, then discard. Add the wine and bring to a simmer.

3. Gradually add the cheese mixture, stirring constantly. Add the aquavit and cook until the cheese is melted and thick, 5 to 8 minutes.

4. Season with plenty of ground pepper and a pinch of nutmeg. Transfer the fondue to a pot over a Sterno flame. Serve immediately with your choice of dipping ingredients.

SPRING
Smorgasbord Brunch Menu

Bootlegger Jell-O Shots 168

Rhubarb Lemonade 171

Gravlax 172

Norwegian Rye Bread 88

Flatbrød 89

Smorgasbord 175

Lemon Pound Cake with Berries 210

Almond Kringle 10

Bootlegger Jell-O Shots

Makes 64

As the story goes, the Bootlegger cocktail was created by the Minnesota country club set during Prohibition to mask the taste of harsh bathtub gin. The original recipe uses frozen limeade and lemonade for a refreshing (and strong!) summer libation, but for this version I added a classic Midwestern ingredient: Jell-O. Try them for your next party—they're sure to be a hit!

MINT SIMPLE SYRUP

½ cup sugar

½ cup water

½ cup packed mint leaves

JELL-O SHOTS

1 cup gin

½ cup cold or room-temperature water

¼ cup lemon juice

½ cup lime juice

3 ounces (3 packets) unflavored gelatin

1 cup boiling water

DIRECTIONS

1. **MAKE THE SIMPLE SYRUP:** Place the sugar and water in a small saucepan. Bring to a simmer over medium heat, stirring until the sugar dissolves. Remove from the heat and add the mint to the pot. Let cool for at least 1 hour, or cover and refrigerate for up to 1 day. The longer you let it sit, the stronger the mint flavor will be. Strain and discard the mint leaves.

2. **MAKE THE JELL-O SHOTS:** Lightly coat an 8-by-8 or 9-by-9-inch square pan with baking spray.

3. Stir together the cooled simple syrup, gin, water, lemon juice, and lime juice in a large bowl. Sprinkle the gelatin packets over the mixture and let sit for 5 minutes, until softened.

4. Pour the boiling water over the gelatin mixture and stir until the gelatin is dissolved.

5. Pour into the prepared pan. Refrigerate until set, at least 4 hours or overnight.

6. To serve, cut into 1-inch squares. Carefully flip onto a serving platter, or use a spatula to remove from the pan. Keep chilled until ready to serve.

Rhubarb Lemonade

Makes about 3 cups

Rhubarb's tart flavor adds a delicious tang to homemade lemonade in this refreshing springtime drink—or try it spiked with gin or vodka for adults-only gatherings! The syrup will keep for a few months in the refrigerator, so you can make a batch during rhubarb season to have on hand for future gatherings. It's also delicious on its own or stirred into cocktails.

RHUBARB SYRUP

1 pound rhubarb, chopped (about 4 cups)

1 cup water

¾ cup sugar

LEMONADE

2 cups lemon juice (from about 10 large lemons)

½ to ¾ cup sugar

Still or sparkling water to taste

DIRECTIONS

1. **MAKE THE RHUBARB SYRUP:** Line a sieve or colander with cheesecloth and place over a medium bowl.

2. Place the rhubarb and water in a large saucepan over medium-high heat. Bring to a boil, then reduce the heat to low and simmer for 30 minutes. Do not stir. Pour into the prepared sieve over the bowl. Strain for 1 hour, then squeeze all the liquid from the cheesecloth into the bowl. Discard solids in cheesecloth.

3. Return the liquid to the saucepan and add the sugar. Bring to a simmer over medium heat, stirring to dissolve the sugar. Let cool and transfer to a covered container. The syrup can be refrigerated for up to 3 months.

4. **TO MAKE THE LEMONADE:** Stir the lemon juice and ½ cup sugar together in a large pitcher or jar. Add up to ¼ cup more sugar if desired. For 1 drink, add ½ cup of the lemon juice mixture and 2 tablespoons rhubarb syrup to an ice-filled glass. Fill with still or sparkling water (I like about ¾ cup water, but you can try different proportions). For a crowd, add the rhubarb syrup to the lemon juice mixture in a pitcher. Stir with a few cups of ice, then add 4 cups still or sparkling water.

Gravlax

Makes 3 pounds

When I lived in New York City, I was introduced to the delights of Russ & Daughters, the iconic "appetizing store" on the Lower East Side, and most importantly, to their top-notch cured fish. When I came home for Christmas, I would always have a supply of bagels, lox, and cream cheese stowed in my suitcase.

While the options for purchasing Jewish delicacies in the Twin Cities are unfortunately limited, there is plenty of overlap between Eastern European Jewish immigrants and my Norwegian and Swedish ancestors in their love of cured fish. Lox and gravlax use the same technique of curing salmon with salt and sugar, but Scandinavian gravlax adds plenty of dill and sometimes other spices such as coriander, juniper, or horseradish.

We now make gravlax as the centerpiece of our family's annual smorgasbord brunch to celebrate my dad's birthday, and I always freeze a couple of smaller fillets to have on hand for impromptu celebrations (or just a good bagel) year-round. I learned the brining trick from Lynda Marren, a mentor and manager I worked with for years in California, and it's an essential first step in adding flavor and maintaining the appearance of your salmon.

⅓ cup kosher salt, plus more for brine

One 3-pound skin-on, sushi-grade salmon fillet

1 tablespoon coriander seeds

1 teaspoon black peppercorns

1 tablespoon sugar

1 large bunch dill, roughly chopped

5 bay leaves, preferably fresh

Pumpernickel or rye bread, Flatbrød
   (page 89), or bagels for serving

Cream cheese or horseradish cream for serving

DIRECTIONS

1. Fill a large bowl or 9-by-13-inch baking dish with cold water. Add a few tablespoons of salt and stir to dissolve. Add the salmon and brine for 10 minutes. This helps add to the flavor and firm texture, and gets rid of the white protein that can form on salmon when cooked or cured. (You can do this before roasting or sautéing salmon as well.)

2. Crush the coriander seeds and peppercorns in a mortar and pestle or spice grinder.

Place in a small bowl and mix with ⅓ cup salt and the sugar.

3. Remove the salmon from the brine and pat dry with paper towels. Lay half of the dill in a 9-by-13-inch baking dish. Place the salmon over the dill in the baking dish. Pat the salt mixture all over the skin, top, and sides of the salmon. Scatter the remaining dill over the salmon and lay the bay leaves on top. Cover with plastic wrap. Place a smaller dish (I use a large loaf pan) weighted with cans or pie weights on top of the salmon. Refrigerate for at least 48 hours and up to 72 hours. Flip the salmon once per day, re-covering with plastic wrap and weights.

4. To serve, place the salmon on a work surface. Scrape off the dill and discard the bay leaves. Use a very sharp knife to cut thin slices at a 45-degree angle. Gravlax can be tightly wrapped and refrigerated for up to 5 days, or freeze for up to 3 months.

Smorgasbord

Serves 8 to 10

My family started serving a smorgasbord brunch to celebrate my dad's birthday a decade ago—because his birthday is on Christmas Eve and we always gather with extended family that evening, it's a way to dedicate part of the inevitably busy day just to him. It's now become a tradition, and a smorgasbord draws on some of the aspects I love most about entertaining. You can't help but be enticed by a big spread of cheese, meat, fish, vegetables, and bread, and each person can pick and choose what they like, trying out different combinations over a leisurely meal.

While a smorgasbord is defined by the spread of ingredients, this meal is all about the smørrebrød: the Danish open-faced sandwich that's popular at breakfast, lunch, and dinner. The combinations can include anything from butter, pickled herring, and radishes, to roast beef and pickles, to cream cheese, gravlax, and cherry tomatoes. I've listed a few suggestions below to get you started, but the possibilities are endless!

Gravlax (page 172), lox, or cold-smoked salmon

Pickled herring

Poached shrimp

Salmon or trout roe

Cured meats, such as prosciutto, salami, or cured ham

Roast beef, thinly sliced

A variety of soft and hard cheeses

Hard-boiled eggs, sliced lengthwise

Norwegian Rye Bread (page 88), or rye and/or pumpernickel bread

Flatbrød (page 89) or rye crackers

Crackers

Mustard

Cream cheese

Butter

Horseradish

Sliced avocado

Pickled vegetables, such as Refrigerator Pickles (page 113) or Quick Pickled Shallots (page 39)

Sliced red onions

Cherry tomatoes

Sliced cucumbers

Roasted asparagus

Radishes

Edible flowers

Sprouts, watercress, or arugula

Dill

Lemon

SMØRREBRØD SUGGESTIONS (SERVE OPEN-FACED ON RYE BREAD)

Butter, hard-boiled eggs, salmon roe

Cream cheese, horseradish, gravlax, cucumbers

Mustard, roast beef, pickles

Avocado, poached shrimp, squeeze of lemon

Cured ham, cheese, roasted asparagus

Butter, pickled herring, dill, sliced red onion

SUMMER
Midsummer Kräftskiva Menu

Scandinavian Sangria 179

Hot Salmon Dip 36

Kräftskiva 180

Tomato Salad with Crispy
Rye Bread Crumbs 59

Angel Food Cake with Whipped Crème
Fraîche & Strawberries 194

Scandinavian Sangria

Serves 8 to 10

Sangria is definitively not a traditional Scandinavian—or Midwestern—drink, but when paired with aquavit's nuanced herbal flavor, it's the perfect base for a refreshing summer cocktail. This combination plays up the spirit's savory notes with the uncomplicated sweetness of local berries, elderflower, and crisp white wine.

1½ cups aquavit

½ cup elderflower syrup or liqueur (see Notes)

2 cups raspberries

2 cups blackberries

2 sprigs rosemary, plus more for garnish if desired

Two 750-ml bottles dry white wine, such as sauvignon blanc

3 cups club soda, chilled

DIRECTIONS

1. In a large pitcher, combine the aquavit, elderflower syrup, raspberries, blackberries, and rosemary. Muddle for a few seconds with a muddler or wooden spoon to release the oils. Pour the wine over the mixture. Stir, cover, and refrigerate for at least 4 hours or overnight.

2. Add the club soda to the pitcher and serve, spooning berries into each glass and garnishing with a small sprig of rosemary, if desired.

Notes

Elderflower syrup is available at specialty grocery stores, or you can find it at Ikea or World Market. Elderflower liqueur is widely available at liquor stores—the most common brand is St-Germain.

This sangria is not particularly sweet, so if you prefer a sweeter drink, macerate ½ cup sugar with the fruit in step 1.

Kräftskiva (Swedish Crawfish or Shrimp Boil)

Serves 8

Crawfish boils are popular at midsummer in Sweden, as well as across the American South. For this recipe, I combined the two traditions, imparting Scandinavian flavors such as dill, caraway, and stout beer to a Cajun-influenced spice mix. Crawfish are also commonly found in Minnesotan ponds and lakes, and my sisters and I often caught them in the pond behind our house growing up (though we were too squeamish to eat them!).

KRÄFTSKIVA

- 1½ gallons water (192 ounces)
- Two 12-ounce bottles stout beer, such as Guinness
- 1 cup kosher salt
- 3 tablespoons sugar
- 2 bay leaves
- 1 bunch dill
- 1 tablespoon black peppercorns
- 1 tablespoon cayenne
- 1 tablespoon paprika
- 1 tablespoon coriander seeds
- 1 tablespoon onion powder
- 1 tablespoon fennel seeds
- 1 tablespoon caraway seeds
- 4 pounds live crawfish or head-on shrimp, cleaned
- 3 pounds red new potatoes, cut in half if large
- 6 ears corn, husked and halved

LEMONY MAYONNAISE

- 2 garlic cloves
- Pinch of kosher salt
- 2 egg yolks
- ¼ cup lemon juice
- ¾ cup olive oil
- ¾ cup canola oil
- 1 tablespoon lemon zest

TO SERVE

- Dill sprigs
- Lemon wedges
- Sliced grilled bread
- Hard cheeses
- Green salad
- Southern hot sauce, such as Tabasco

DIRECTIONS

1. **PREPARE THE CRAWFISH:** Add the water, beer, salt, sugar, bay leaves, dill, peppercorns, cayenne, paprika, coriander, onion powder, fennel seeds, and caraway seeds, to a large pot. Cover and bring to a boil.

2. Add the crawfish to the pot, cover, and return to a boil. Reduce the heat and simmer, stirring occasionally, until the crawfish are bright red, 5 to 10 minutes (1 to 2 minutes for shrimp). Remove from the heat and refrigerate, keeping the ingredients in the pot, for at least 6 hours or overnight. Cover the pot once the brine has cooled.

3. **MAKE THE LEMONY MAYONNAISE:** Mince the garlic, adding a pinch of salt as you chop until it forms a rough paste. Add the garlic to a medium bowl and whisk in

CONTINUED ▶

the egg yolks. Whisk in 1 teaspoon of the lemon juice (this helps keep the mayo stable).

4. Combine the olive and canola oils in a measuring cup with a spout or a small pitcher. Slowly add the oils in a very slow stream to the egg, whisking constantly or using a hand blender. Alternatively, place the garlic, salt, egg, and lemon juice in a food processor or blender and add the oils in a slow stream while blending.

5. The mixture will be very creamy and thick. Add the remaining lemon juice and the zest, and salt to taste. Refrigerate for up to 1 week.

6. **TO SERVE:** Using a skimmer or slotted spoon, remove the crawfish from the pot and place on a platter. Bring the broth in the pot to a boil. Add the new potatoes to the broth and cook for 10 to 12 minutes. Add the corn and cook for 5 to 8 minutes, until the vegetables are tender. Drain.

7. Spread the vegetables on newspaper spread on a table. Place the crawfish over the vegetables. Garnish with dill sprigs. Serve with lemony mayo, cut lemons, grilled bread, hard cheeses, salad, and hot sauce. (And beer and aquavit!)

FALL
Maple-Glazed Ham Buffet Menu

Lingonberry Old-Fashioned 186

Norwegian Potato Balls 40

Maple-Glazed Ham 189

Speedy Homemade Rolls 92

Scalloped Corn 106

Cabbage Salad with Caraway Seeds 56

Refrigerator Pickles 113

Scalloped Potatoes 117

Apple Cake 197

Lingonberry Old-Fashioned

Serves 1

Though difficult to find in their raw form, lingonberries are a staple in Scandinavian cuisine and are served with everything from braised meats to waffles. Their tart, tannic flavor is a natural pairing with smoky whiskey in this autumnal take on the old-fashioned. It's a perfect holiday cocktail to sip by a roaring fire—or at least, one of the many yule log videos on YouTube. My sister Solveig tested this recipe for me, and she had the genius idea to stir in a little ground pepper—it adds amazing depth and flavor. For a crowd, make a pitcher ahead of time by multiplying the recipe by 10, then strain over ice.

2 teaspoons lingonberry jam (see Note)

1 teaspoon hot water

⅛ to ¼ teaspoon honey

3 dashes Angostura bitters

Crack of freshly ground pepper

2 ounces whiskey

Orange peel for garnish

DIRECTIONS

1. Add a large ice cube to a rocks glass or fill halfway with ice.

2. Add the lingonberry jam, water, honey, bitters, and pepper to a cocktail shaker. Muddle to combine and crush the lingonberries. Fill a cocktail shaker with ice and add the whiskey. Shake until cold, 10 to 15 seconds. Use a fine mesh sieve or the top of the cocktail shaker to strain the cocktail into the prepared glass.

3. Run the orange peel around the rim of the glass, then drop into the glass. Serve immediately.

Note

You can find lingonberry jam at Ikea, well-stocked grocery stores, or online.

Maple-Glazed Ham

Serves 16 to 20

Ham is an ideal party food. It was always the centerpiece of my family's Easter brunch, and my parents would often serve one in addition to roast turkey at our large Thanksgiving gatherings. Though my grandma Veola always made the classic pineapple and clove-studded ham, I like to use a mixture of spiced maple syrup, vinegar, and bourbon for a sweet-and-sour glaze. Serve with Speedy Homemade Rolls (page 92) or store-bought potato rolls and plenty of butter and mustard. Pickles are optional but highly encouraged.

One 12- to 15-pound whole bone-in ham, at room temperature

1½ cups maple syrup

1-inch piece fresh ginger, thinly sliced

1 tablespoon orange zest

1 tablespoon fennel seeds, crushed

1½ teaspoons coriander seeds, crushed

1 teaspoon whole black peppercorns, crushed

6 whole cloves

4 star anise

3 garlic cloves, thinly sliced

2 dried red chiles or ½ teaspoon red pepper flakes

1 cup bourbon or rye whiskey

1 cup chicken stock or water

½ cup apple cider vinegar

2 tablespoons soy sauce

DIRECTIONS

1. Preheat oven to 325°F. Place ham fat side up in a large roasting dish and add 1 cup water. Use a sharp knife to score the skin in a crosshatch pattern. Cover with foil and roast for 1½ hours.

2. Meanwhile, place the maple syrup in a large saucepan. Bring to a boil over medium-high heat. Add the ginger, orange zest, fennel, coriander, black pepper, cloves, star anise, garlic, and chiles. Cook for 30 seconds, until fragrant. Carefully add the bourbon, chicken stock, vinegar, and soy sauce. Bring to a simmer and cook for 15 to 20 minutes, until reduced by about one-quarter. Strain through a fine mesh sieve and discard spices.

3. After 1½ hours, uncover and baste the ham with the pan juices. Brush the maple syrup glaze over the ham. Repeat every 15 minutes, until the top of the ham is golden brown and caramelized and an instant read thermometer reads 130°F when inserted into the thickest part, 1½ to 2 hours more.

4. Transfer the ham to a cutting board and rest for 15 minutes. Skim the fat from the pan juices and transfer the juices to a serving bowl. Carve the ham as desired and serve with the pan juices.

DESSERTS

I don't have any formal pastry training, but desserts have always been a big part of my life.

My mom and sisters are all avid and talented bakers, and my first job was at a bakery assisting with the production of muffins, croissants, and scones. It's all but guaranteed that any Midwestern gathering will include an array of desserts, often a spread of bars and cookies accompanied by a big carafe of freshly brewed coffee.

In this chapter, you'll find recipes for a variety of bars, cookies, cakes, and pie. Most use one bowl and are easy to prepare in under a couple of hours—while I love a good baking project, I prefer simpler desserts for everyday consumption. One thing I learned while working on the recipes in this book: Don't be afraid of lard! It adds incredible flaky texture to piecrust and cookies, and imparts a just-slightly savory quality to sweets that I absolutely love. Many of my grandmothers' recipes used lard as the primary fat in baked goods (in those days, it was easier and cheaper to procure than butter), but I prefer a mix of butter and lard for the best flavor and texture. You can find lard at your local butcher shop, or in the meat department of your grocery store. Of course, if you're a vegetarian, you can simply use all butter instead.

A couple of recipes in this chapter may be less familiar to those who didn't grow up in the Midwest: Pomegranate & Berry Jell-O Salad (page 220) and Apple Candy Bar Salad (page 198). *Salads,* you may be thinking, *in a dessert chapter?* Hear me out: Traditionally, these "salads" (so-called because they contain fruit) were served as part of the main meal or lunch buffet, right alongside ham sandwiches and potato salad. We eat a little differently now though, so in my book they fall firmly in the sweets category. These dessert salad dishes are slightly more sophisticated versions of the ones I loved so much growing up, though if you use boxed Jell-O mix and Snickers bars instead of fruit juice and chopped dark chocolate, I certainly understand. Sometimes, there's no need to mess with a classic.

Angel Food Cake with Whipped Crème Fraîche & Strawberries

Serves 6 to 8

My grandma Veola made angel food cake with strawberries and whipped cream for nearly every special occasion, and it's one of the desserts I associate most strongly with my childhood. Whipping cream with crème fraîche adds stability as well as flavor, so you can assemble the cake a few hours before serving.

ANGEL FOOD CAKE

1 cup plus 2 tablespoons cake flour (see Note)

¾ cup granulated sugar

1⅓ cups egg whites (from about 12 large eggs)

½ teaspoon kosher salt

1½ teaspoons cream of tartar

¾ cup powdered sugar

1 teaspoon vanilla extract

1 teaspoon almond extract

1 pound strawberries, hulled and sliced

WHIPPED CRÈME FRAÎCHE

2 cups heavy whipping cream

½ cup crème fraîche

2 tablespoons to ¼ cup granulated sugar

½ teaspoon vanilla extract

DIRECTIONS

1. Preheat oven to 375°F. Butter and flour three 9-inch cake pans and line with parchment paper rounds. Set aside.

2. **MAKE THE CAKE:** Sift the flour with the sugar into a medium bowl, repeating two or three times until no lumps remain. Add the egg whites and salt to the bowl of a stand mixer fitted with the whisk attachment and beat on high until foamy, about 1 minute. Add the cream of tartar and turn the mixer on high. Gradually add the powdered sugar to the running mixer, beating until stiff peaks form, 3 to 4 minutes. Beat in the vanilla and almond extracts until just combined. Gently fold in the flour and sugar mixture with a spatula until almost completely combined—you may have a few dry spots.

3. Divide the batter between the prepared pans and smooth the tops. Bake for 25 to 30 minutes, until light golden brown and the cake springs back when you press it gently. Remove the cakes from the pans and let cool completely on a rack.

4. **MAKE THE WHIPPED CRÈME FRAÎCHE:** Add the whipping cream, crème fraîche, 2 tablespoons to ¼ cup sugar (depending on how sweet you like it), and vanilla to the bowl of a stand mixer and beat on medium-low speed until soft peaks form, 2 to 3 minutes. Refrigerate until ready to use.

5. **TO ASSEMBLE:** Place one cake layer on a serving plate. Spread one-third of the whipped crème fraîche over the cake. Place strawberry slices in concentric circles over the whipped cream. Repeat with the remaining layers, ending with whipped cream and strawberries. Decorate the top of the cake as desired. The cake can be made up to 3 hours before serving. Refrigerate until ready to serve.

Note

If you don't have cake flour on hand (which I almost never do), you can make an easy substitute at home: Measure out 1 cup all-purpose flour and remove 2 tablespoons. Replace with 2 tablespoons cornstarch.

Apple Cake

Serves 6 to 8

Using a combination of butter and oil in this one-bowl cake adds wonderful flavor and makes the texture extra moist, and it has become a favorite of ours as a sweet end to dinner on Rosh Hashanah. Be sure to use firm apples that will hold their shape while baking, such as Gala, Cortland, or Braeburn.

2½ cups all-purpose flour

2 teaspoons cinnamon

1½ teaspoons kosher salt

1 teaspoon baking powder

½ teaspoon baking soda

¾ cup (1½ sticks) unsalted butter, softened

1½ cups granulated sugar

½ cup vegetable or canola oil

2 eggs

1 tablespoon vanilla extract

4 medium apples (such as Gala), peeled and cored

Powdered sugar for serving

DIRECTIONS

1. Preheat oven to 350°F. Lightly grease a 9-inch springform or round pan.

2. Mix the flour, cinnamon, salt, baking powder, and baking soda in a medium bowl.

3. Place the butter and sugar in the bowl of a stand mixer fitted with the paddle attachment. Beat on medium until light and fluffy, 2 to 3 minutes. Add the oil and eggs, one at a time, beating until blended. Add the vanilla and beat to blend.

4. Slowly add the dry ingredients to the batter, beating on low until mostly mixed. Remove the bowl from the mixer.

5. Cut 2 of the apples into ½-inch pieces and stir into the cake batter. Cut the remaining 2 apples in half. Cut each half into thin wedges, keeping the wedges together.

6. Spread the batter in the prepared pan (it will be thick). Arrange the wedges on top of the batter.

7. Bake until a tester inserted in the center comes out clean, 70 to 80 minutes, depending on the water content of your fruit.

8. Let the cake cool on a rack for 15 minutes. Run a knife around the edge, then remove the springform edge if using a springform pan. Alternatively, flip the cake onto a plate, then flip it right side up. Transfer the cake to a serving platter and cool completely.

9. Sprinkle with powdered sugar and serve.

Apple Candy Bar Salad

Serves 4 to 6

I'm taking some liberties with the term "salad" here, though if you grew up in the upper Midwest, you are no doubt familiar with salads that include Jell-O, cookies, and even candy bars. This dish was a staple on my family's Easter buffet, and it was always a hit with all the kids for obvious reasons. The original version consists of sliced Granny Smith apples, Cool Whip, and chopped Snickers bars (and if you want to use Snickers bars instead of dark chocolate here, I certainly won't stop you!). The key? Make sure your chocolate, cream, and apples are chilled ahead of time to get the maximum texture and flavor contrast between the crisp apples and whipped cream.

1 cup heavy whipping cream, chilled

¼ cup sour cream, chilled

2 tablespoons sugar

½ teaspoon vanilla extract

4 Granny Smith apples, chilled, cored, cut into ½-inch pieces

3 to 4 ounces dark chocolate, chopped

½ cup homemade or prepared caramel sauce

¼ cup chopped salted peanuts

DIRECTIONS

1. Combine the whipping cream, sour cream, sugar, and vanilla in a medium bowl or the bowl of a stand mixer fitted with the whisk attachment. Beat on medium-low speed until soft peaks form, about 3 minutes.

2. Combine the apples, whipped cream mixture, and half of the chocolate in a serving bowl and stir to coat. Drizzle caramel sauce over the apple mixture, then top with the remaining dark chocolate and peanuts. Serve immediately or refrigerate for up to 2 hours.

Apple Crisp

Serves 6 to 8

My mom makes this crisp at least every other week in the fall, and it's a wonderful and easy way to use up that bag of apples you picked in an overzealous trip to the orchard. This recipe is adapted from the original created by my aunt Jill's mother-in-law, Kathleen, whose family had a number of apple trees on their farm. In my family we love the simplicity of the buttery crisp, but you could certainly mix in ½ cup rolled oats for a crunchier topping. Serve with freshly whipped cream or homemade Vanilla Ice Cream (page 227). If you have leftovers, serve it for breakfast with a little Greek yogurt.

1 cup all-purpose flour

¾ cup sugar

½ teaspoon kosher salt

½ cup (1 stick) unsalted butter, room temperature

6 firm apples, such as Honeycrisp, Gala, or Jonagold, peeled, cored, and thinly sliced

1 teaspoon cinnamon

¼ teaspoon nutmeg

DIRECTIONS

1. Heat oven to 375°F. Butter an 8-by-8-inch square baking dish or a 9-inch round cake pan.

2. For the topping, mix the flour, sugar, and salt together in a large bowl. Add the butter and mix until creamy and well combined. Set aside.

3. Spread the apples in the prepared pan—they should reach nearly to the top. Sprinkle evenly with the cinnamon and nutmeg. Spread the topping in an even layer over the apples, pressing down onto the apples and into the cracks. Bake for 45 to 55 minutes, until the apples are bubbling and the topping is golden brown and crispy. Let cool for 15 minutes before serving. Serve warm or at room temperature.

Brown Butterscotch Blondies

Makes 24 blondies

My dad is allergic to chocolate, so my mom was always looking for non-cocoa-based desserts to bake for him when I was a kid. We would often make a pan of blondies for an easy afternoon treat on the weekends. These days, I love a blondie with a dense, chewy texture and butterscotch flavor—and these certainly fit the bill thanks to the brown sugar and homemade butterscotch drizzle. Save any extra butterscotch sauce to serve with ice cream.

BUTTERSCOTCH SAUCE

¼ cup (½ stick) unsalted butter

⅓ cup packed brown sugar

½ cup heavy whipping cream

½ teaspoon kosher salt

1 teaspoon vanilla extract

BLONDIES

1 cup (2 sticks) unsalted butter

2½ cups lightly packed brown sugar

2 eggs

2 teaspoons vanilla extract

2½ cups all-purpose flour

1 teaspoon baking powder

¾ teaspoon kosher salt

Flaky sea salt, such as Maldon, for sprinkling

DIRECTIONS

1. **MAKE THE BUTTERSCOTCH SAUCE:** Melt the butter in a small saucepan over medium heat. Cook until the butter browns and smells nutty, about 5 minutes. Add the brown sugar, whipping cream, and salt and whisk until combined. Cook for about 5 minutes, until the mixture thickens and begins to caramelize. Remove from the heat and whisk in 1 teaspoon vanilla. Set aside.

2. **MAKE THE BLONDIES:** Preheat oven to 350°F. Butter a 9-by-13-inch baking dish or spray with baking spray.

3. Melt the butter in a small saucepan over medium heat. Cook until the butter browns and smells nutty, 5 to 8 minutes. Pour into a large bowl, scraping up all the browned bits at the bottom of the pan.

4. Whisk the brown sugar, eggs, and vanilla into the browned butter until combined. Add the flour, baking powder, and salt and whisk to combine.

5. Spread the batter (it will be thick) in the prepared pan. Drizzle the butterscotch sauce over the blondies, dragging with a toothpick or skewer to distribute the sauce.

6. Bake the blondies until golden brown and a tester inserted in the middle comes out clean, 20 to 25 minutes. Let cool for 5 minutes, then sprinkle with flaky salt. Cool completely and cut into squares. Store in an airtight container for up to 1 week.

Cardamom Stone Fruit Cobbler

Serves 6 to 8

For this tasty summer dessert, cardamom imparts warmth and complexity to sweet stone fruit. I have also made it with a mixture of strawberries, blackberries, and raspberries, which is equally delicious. Serve with freshly whipped cream or homemade Vanilla Ice Cream (page 227) as the finale to an August dinner party alfresco.

BUTTERMILK BISCUITS

2 cups flour, plus more for dusting

¼ cup sugar

1 tablespoon baking powder

1 teaspoon ground cardamom

¾ teaspoon kosher salt

½ teaspoon baking soda

6 tablespoons unsalted butter, chilled and cut into 1-tablespoon-size pieces

1 cup buttermilk

FRUIT FILLING

4 pounds peaches and plums, pitted and cut into 1-inch pieces

½ cup sugar

2 tablespoons cornstarch

1½ teaspoons ground cardamom

1 teaspoon vanilla extract

½ teaspoon kosher salt

¼ cup heavy cream

DIRECTIONS

1. **MAKE THE BISCUITS:** Mix the flour, sugar, baking powder, cardamom, salt, and baking soda in a large bowl. Add the butter and, working quickly, smash the butter into the flour mixture with your hands or a pastry cutter until you have pea-size pieces. Gradually add the buttermilk, mixing with your hands or a fork as you go, until the mixture comes together to form a shaggy dough.

2. Turn the dough onto a lightly floured surface. Shape into a disc and cover tightly with plastic wrap. Chill for at least 1 hour, and up to 1 day.

3. Roll the chilled biscuit dough to a ¾-inch-thick disc. Use a 2-inch biscuit cutter to cut biscuits as closely together as possible. Reshape the dough scraps and cut as many more biscuits as you can (you should have about 12 total). Transfer the biscuits to a parchment paper–lined baking sheet and chill until ready to use.

4. **MAKE THE FRUIT FILLING:** Preheat oven to 375°F.

5. Mix the peaches and plums, sugar, cornstarch, cardamom, vanilla, and salt in a large bowl. Toss well to combine. Spread the fruit in an even layer in a 9-inch skillet or cake pan. Place the biscuits on top of the fruit, fitting them in as snugly as you can. Place the pan on a rimmed baking sheet. Brush the biscuits with the cream.

6. Bake for 50 to 60 minutes, until the berries are bubbling and the biscuits are golden brown. Let cool for 15 minutes before serving. The cobbler can be baked up to 6 hours ahead.

Chocolate Fudge Cake

Serves 8 to 10

This decadent chocolate cake, credited to Mom Healey in my grandma Veola's recipes, uses a couple of old-school techniques that give it amazing texture and depth of flavor. The hot water and melted chocolate in the cake batter makes it incredibly moist, while using whole eggs in the frosting (instead of a buttercream with cooked egg whites and butter) results in a silky, whipped frosting that's not too sweet. A note: If it's a hot day or your kitchen runs warm, you may need to refrigerate the frosting for longer than 10 minutes for it to whip properly. You're looking for a light yet spreadable texture (not too liquidy). This frosting is pretty forgiving, so don't be afraid to stick it back in the fridge if it doesn't seem to be thickening properly.

FUDGE CAKE

2 cups flour

1¾ cups granulated sugar

½ teaspoon kosher salt

½ cup (1 stick) unsalted butter

½ cup vegetable oil

1 cup hot water

½ cup unsweetened cocoa powder

2 ounces unsweetened chocolate, chopped

1 tablespoon instant espresso powder

½ cup buttermilk

2 eggs

1 teaspoon vanilla extract

1 teaspoon baking soda

WHIPPED CHOCOLATE FROSTING

6 tablespoons unsalted butter

4 ounces unsweetened chocolate, chopped

2 cups powdered sugar

½ cup whole milk, chilled

2 pasteurized eggs, chilled

1 teaspoon vanilla

¼ teaspoon kosher salt

DIRECTIONS

1. **MAKE THE CAKE:** Preheat oven to 350°F. Butter and flour two round 9-inch cake pans or a 9-by-13-inch baking dish. Line the pans with parchment paper rounds, or if using a baking dish, line with a piece of parchment paper large enough to hang over the long sides.

2. Mix the flour, sugar, and salt together in a large bowl. Set aside.

3. Place the butter, oil, hot water, cocoa powder, chocolate, and espresso powder in a small saucepan. Whisk over medium heat until the butter is melted and the mixture comes to a boil, about 3 minutes. Pour over the flour mixture in the bowl and whisk to combine.

4. Add the buttermilk, eggs, vanilla, and baking soda to the batter. Whisk until fully combined.

5. Divide the batter between the cake pans, or pour into the 9-by-13-inch baking dish. Bake for 30 minutes, until a tester inserted in the middle comes out clean. Turn the cakes onto a wire rack to cool completely.

6. **MAKE THE WHIPPED CHOCOLATE FROSTING:** Melt the butter and chocolate in a small saucepan over low heat. Remove from the heat and cool for 5 minutes.

7. Place the powdered sugar, milk, eggs, vanilla, and salt in the bowl of a stand mixer and mix to combine. Add the melted butter mixture and mix on low to combine.

8. Remove the bowl from the mixer and refrigerate for 10 to 20 minutes, until the frosting has begun to firm up. After 10 minutes, return the bowl to the mixer and beat on medium-high speed until light and fluffy, about 5 minutes. Note: If it's a warm day or your kitchen is particularly warm, you may need to refrigerate the frosting for longer than 10 minutes. If it's not thickening, refrigerate in 10-minute increments and try whipping again. When whipped, it should be thick, spreadable, and fluffy.

9. To assemble the layer cake, place one cake layer top side down on a serving plate. Spread 1 cup frosting over the top of the cake. Place the remaining layer over the frosting. Use an offset spatula to spread the remaining frosting over the top and sides of cake, swirling decoratively if desired.

Lemon Bars

Makes 24 bars

My mom often made a version of these to bring to potlucks and holiday gatherings when I was growing up, even though she doesn't like lemon! They're my dad's favorite. I punched up the lemony flavor by adding some zest and an additional egg yolk to the filling.

CRUST

2 cups all-purpose flour

¼ cup sugar

1 tablespoon cornstarch

½ teaspoon kosher salt

1 cup (2 sticks) unsalted butter, softened

FILLING

4 eggs

1 egg yolk

2 cups sugar

¼ cup flour

1 teaspoon baking powder

¼ teaspoon kosher salt

⅓ cup lemon juice

2 tablespoons lemon zest

GLAZE

1 cup powdered sugar

2 to 3 tablespoons lemon juice

DIRECTIONS

1. Preheat oven to 350°F. Spray a 9-by-13-inch baking dish with baking spray or coat with butter and set aside.

2. **MAKE THE CRUST:** Combine the flour, sugar, cornstarch, and salt in the bowl of a stand mixer fitted with the paddle attachment. Add the butter and beat until combined, about 1 minute.

3. Press the crust in an even layer onto the bottom of the prepared pan. Bake for 20 to 30 minutes, until golden brown.

4. **MAKE THE FILLING:** When the bars are cooled, whisk the eggs, yolk, sugar, flour, baking powder, and salt together in a large bowl. Whisk in the lemon juice and zest.

5. Pour the filling over the warm crust. Bake for 25 to 30 minutes, until the top is crispy and light golden brown. Cool completely.

6. **MAKE THE GLAZE:** When the bars are cooled, whisk the powdered sugar and 2 tablespoons lemon juice together in a small bowl until no lumps remain. Add more lemon juice as needed for a drizzling consistency.

7. Drizzle the glaze over the bars in the pan, then cut into 1½-inch squares and serve.

Lemon Pound Cake with Berries

Makes one 9-by-5-inch loaf

This easy one-bowl cake comes together quickly, but a word of caution: Make sure your ingredients are fully at room temperature before mixing! If they're not, the cake may end up dense and dry. If you like, skip the berries and whipped cream and serve this cake for breakfast, or try with peaches or plums in the summer.

LEMON POUND CAKE

2½ cups cake flour (see Note on page 195)

1½ teaspoons baking powder

½ teaspoon baking soda

½ teaspoon kosher salt

1 cup (2 sticks) unsalted butter, room temperature

1 cup granulated sugar

2 tablespoons lemon zest

1 teaspoon vanilla extract

2 eggs, room temperature

½ cup buttermilk, room temperature

GLAZE

½ cup granulated sugar

2 tablespoons lemon juice

1 tablespoon water

BERRIES

3 cups mixed berries, such as strawberries, raspberries, blackberries, or currants

2 tablespoons granulated sugar

1 tablespoon lemon zest

WHIPPED CREAM

2 cups heavy whipping cream

¼ cup granulated sugar

1 teaspoon vanilla extract

DIRECTIONS

1. **MAKE THE POUND CAKE:** Preheat oven to 350°F. Coat a 9-by-5-inch loaf pan with baking spray and line with parchment paper.

2. Sift the cake flour, baking powder, baking soda, and salt together in a medium bowl. Set aside.

3. Place the butter in the bowl of a stand mixer fitted with the paddle attachment. Beat on medium speed for 2 minutes. With the mixer running on low, add the sugar, then beat on medium speed until light and fluffy, about 2 minutes more. Add the lemon zest, vanilla, and eggs one at a time, beating after each addition. Add the flour mixture alternately with the buttermilk in two additions each, beating after each addition until just combined.

4. Pour the batter into the prepared pan. Bake for 45 to 55 minutes, until a tester inserted in the middle comes out clean. Cool the cake in the pan for 10 minutes. Use a skewer to poke holes in the cake.

5. **MAKE THE GLAZE:** Combine the sugar, lemon juice, and water in a small saucepan. Cook over low heat until the mixture comes to a boil and the sugar is dissolved. Pour the hot syrup over the hot cake in the pan. Let

CONTINUED ▶

stand 1 minute, then loosen the cake around the edges of the pan and carefully remove from the pan. Cool completely on a rack.

6. **MAKE THE BERRIES:** While the cake cools, combine the berries, sugar, and lemon zest in a large bowl. Let sit at room temperature for at least 20 minutes and up to 1 hour, until the berries have begun to macerate and release juices.

7. **MAKE THE WHIPPED CREAM:** Combine the whipping cream, sugar, and vanilla in a medium bowl or the bowl of a stand mixer fitted with the whisk attachment. Beat on medium-low speed until soft peaks form, about 3 minutes.

8. Cut the cake into slices and serve with the berries and whipped cream.

Orange Poppy Seed Cake

Makes one 10-inch Bundt cake or two 8-by-5-inch loaves

This pretty tea cake isn't too sweet, making it ideal to serve as part of a brunch spread or as a light dessert after lunch. Try blood oranges for a pretty, vibrant color! You can also use grapefruit for a more citrusy flavor—just add another ¼ cup sugar. Poppy seeds are often found in Scandinavian baked goods, particularly those of Danish origin, and they add lovely texture to this delicate cake.

ORANGE POPPY SEED CAKE

3 cups all-purpose flour

¼ cup poppy seeds

1½ teaspoons baking powder

1 teaspoon kosher salt

2 cups granulated sugar

¼ cup orange zest

1 cup (2 sticks) unsalted butter, room temperature

3 eggs, room temperature

¼ cup orange juice

1 teaspoon vanilla extract

1 teaspoon almond extract

1½ cups sour cream, room temperature

GLAZE

1¾ cups powdered sugar

¼ cup orange juice

1 tablespoon unsalted butter, melted

½ teaspoon almond extract

Pinch of kosher salt

DIRECTIONS

1. Preheat oven to 350°F. Butter and flour a Bundt pan or two 8-by-5-inch loaf pans.

2. Mix the flour, poppy seeds, baking powder, and salt in a medium bowl. Set aside.

3. Place the sugar and orange zest in the bowl of a stand mixer fitted with the paddle attachment. Use your fingers to rub the zest and sugar together to release the oils. Add the butter and beat on medium speed until light and fluffy, about 3 minutes. Add the eggs one at a time, beating after each addition. Beat in the orange juice, vanilla, and almond extract.

4. Starting with the flour mixture, alternately add the dry ingredients and sour cream in three additions each. Mix on low until the flour is incorporated and the batter is smooth.

5. Scoop the batter into the prepared pan and smooth the top. Bake for 1 hour, until a tester inserted in the middle comes out clean. Cool on a rack for 10 minutes, then turn onto a rack to cool completely.

6. **MAKE THE GLAZE:** Whisk the powdered sugar, orange juice, butter, and almond extract together in a small bowl. Drizzle over the cooled cake. Cut into slices and serve for breakfast or dessert.

Piecrust

Makes 2 discs for a 9-inch pie pan

Though all-butter piecrusts are generally the norm these days, using a little bit of leaf lard adds an incredible flaky texture. Many of my great-grandma Soberg's recipes used lard instead of butter, as it was inexpensive and readily available at the time, but I prefer a mix of the two. For best results, be sure to keep all your ingredients well chilled. If you're making this on a warm day, you should even refrigerate your rolling pin and bowl to keep those flaky pockets of butter intact!

2½ cups all-purpose flour

1 tablespoon sugar

1 teaspoon kosher salt

¾ cup butter (1½ sticks), chilled, cut into 12 pieces

¼ cup leaf lard, chilled (see Note)

Up to ¼ cup ice water

1 tablespoon white or apple cider vinegar

DIRECTIONS

1. Combine the flour, sugar, and salt in a large bowl. Add the butter and lard, and use your fingers to combine into the flour mixture, squishing until the butter and lard are distributed throughout and form pea-size pieces.

2. Combine the ice water and vinegar in a measuring cup or small bowl. Add the liquid to the dough 1 tablespoon at a time, until the dough just starts to come together. Use your hands to knead the dough into a ball, taking care to leave large pieces of fat intact. The dough will still be crumbly.

3. Turn the dough onto a work surface and shape into two discs. Cover tightly with plastic wrap and refrigerate for at least 1 hour or up to 2 days.

4. Remove the dough from the refrigerator 10 to 15 minutes before rolling. Lightly dust your work surface and rolling pin with flour.

5. Using some force, roll the dough outward into a 12-inch, ¼-inch-thick circle. Turn often on the work surface, dusting with flour as needed.

6. Roll the dough onto the rolling pin, then unroll into a 9-inch pie pan. Press the dough into the pan and trim the edge to a 1-inch overhang. Chill until ready to bake. Repeat with the remaining dough disc, and cut into lattice strips or shapes as desired.

Note

If you're making this for vegetarians and/or the Spring Vegetable Hotdish/Potpie (page 94), use 1 cup (2 sticks) butter instead of a combination of butter and lard.

Rhubarb Custard Pie

Makes one 9-inch pie

Rhubarb is in season across the Midwest and East Coast in late spring, and my mom makes this pie at least a few times each spring when their rhubarb plants are ready—and Ari and I have enjoyed a couple of our own since returning to Minnesota. The original recipe comes from my grandma Nancy, and the sweet-tart taste always means that spring has really and truly arrived. While I love the combination of strawberry and rhubarb, the unique custard filling of this pie really allows rhubarb's unique flavor to shine. Serve with whipped cream, homemade Vanilla Ice Cream (page 227), or simply a glass of cold milk.

2 discs Piecrust (page 216) or store-bought piecrust

1½ cups sugar

¼ cup cornstarch

¾ teaspoon ground nutmeg

½ teaspoon kosher salt

3 eggs, lightly beaten

2 teaspoons vanilla extract

5 cups chopped rhubarb (about 1 pound)

2 tablespoons heavy cream

Turbinado or raw sugar for sprinkling

DIRECTIONS

1. Line a rimmed baking sheet with parchment paper. Roll out one disc of the pie dough as directed in the piecrust recipe and line a 9-inch pie pan with the dough circle. Chill until ready to use.

2. **TO MAKE THE LATTICE TOP:** Roll out the remaining dough disc as directed in the recipe. Place the dough circle on the prepared baking sheet. Use a pizza cutter or sharp knife to cut into 1-inch strips (alternatively, cut into different size strips for an uneven lattice pattern). Chill until ready to use.

3. Whisk the sugar, cornstarch, nutmeg, and salt together in a large bowl. Add the eggs and vanilla and whisk until well combined. Stir in the rhubarb until well coated.

4. Remove the pie pan and lattice strips from the refrigerator. Transfer the filling into the pie pan, spreading until even. Working quickly, place a shorter lattice strip along the left edge of the pie. Place another strip perpendicular to the first strip along the top edge. Work toward the opposite edges, alternating strips as you go to create a lattice pattern. Trim the edges of lattice to

CONTINUED ▶

match the edge of the bottom crust, then roll the crust over so it sits along the edge of the pan. Use your thumb and opposite index finger and thumb to pinch the edge of the crust into a crimped pattern. Repeat until the entire edge of the pie is crimped.

5. When ready to bake, preheat oven to 425°F. Brush the top crust with heavy cream and sprinkle with turbinado sugar. Bake the pie for 30 minutes. Cover the edge of the pie-crust with aluminum foil or a pie shield and reduce oven temperature to 375°F. Bake for another 30 to 40 minutes, until the crust is golden brown and the filling is bubbling.

6. Cool for at least 1 hour and up to 8 hours. Cut into wedges.

Pomegranate & Berry Jell-O Salad

Serves 8 to 10

I couldn't *not* include a Jell-O salad in this book, but this version, using real fruit juice and fresh berries, is a far cry from the molded concoctions sold at Midwestern grocery stores. Plus, it's actually kind of gorgeous. Serve it for dessert or as part of a lunch spread to delight adults and kids alike.

6 cups white grape juice

7 ounces (7 packets) unflavored gelatin

3 cups mixed berries, such as raspberries, blackberries, and pomegranate seeds

4 cups pomegranate juice

¼ cup sugar

DIRECTIONS

1. Lightly coat a 12-cup Bundt pan with baking spray.

2. Place 2 cups of the white grape juice in a medium bowl. Sprinkle 4 ounces (4 packets) of the gelatin over the juice in the bowl. Let sit until softened, about 5 minutes.

3. Place the remaining 4 cups white grape juice in a small saucepan. Bring to a boil over medium-high heat. Pour over the gelatin mixture in the bowl and stir to dissolve. Pour into the prepared Bundt pan and sprinkle with the berries. Refrigerate for at least 4 hours, until set.

4. When the berry layer has set, stir together 2 cups of the pomegranate juice and the sugar in a medium bowl. Sprinkle the remaining 3 ounces (3 packets) gelatin over the juice in the bowl. Let sit until softened, about 5 minutes.

5. Place the remaining 2 cups pomegranate juice in a small saucepan. Bring to a boil over medium-high heat. Pour over the gelatin mixture in the bowl and stir to dissolve. Pour over the berry layer in the Bundt pan. Refrigerate for at least 3 hours or overnight.

6. When ready to serve, let the Bundt pan sit at room temperature for 20 minutes. Carefully turn onto a serving platter, and cut into slices. The Jell-O will begin to melt if left at room temperature for too long, so you can also refrigerate it on the serving platter for a few hours.

Sour Cream Sugar Cookies

Makes about 40

These sugar cookies are legendary on my dad's side of the family—they were my great-grandma Soberg's secret recipe, and she never shared it while she was alive. Thankfully, she wrote it down! They really are perfect: The crisp texture and slightly tart taste come from a mixture of butter, lard, and sour cream. It's worth seeking out leaf lard for this recipe, but you can use all butter as well. Believe me, it's hard to limit yourself to just one!

3 cups all-purpose flour, plus more for rolling

½ teaspoon kosher salt

½ teaspoon baking soda

10 tablespoons butter, room temperature

¼ cup lard, room temperature

1½ cups sugar, plus more for sprinkling

2 tablespoons sour cream

2 teaspoons vanilla

2 eggs

DIRECTIONS

1. Sift the flour, salt, and baking soda together in a medium bowl and set aside.

2. Place the butter, lard, and sugar in the bowl of a stand mixer fitted with the paddle attachment. Beat on medium speed until light and fluffy, about 2 minutes. Add the sour cream, vanilla, and eggs, one at a time, beating after each addition. With the mixer running on low, slowly add the dry ingredients until incorporated.

3. Divide the dough in half and form into two discs. Wrap tightly with plastic wrap and chill for at least 1 hour and up to 2 days.

4. When ready to bake, preheat oven to 350°F. Line two rimmed baking sheets with parchment paper. Remove the dough from the refrigerator 10 minutes before rolling out.

5. Sprinkle a work surface lightly with flour. Place the dough on the surface and sprinkle with sugar. Roll ¼ inch thick. Use a 3-inch round cutter to cut the dough into circles. Transfer to the prepared baking sheets, leaving 1 inch between cookies. Sprinkle the rounds liberally with sugar. Reroll the scraps one more time and cut out more cookies. Bake remaining scraps with the rounds.

6. Bake for 10 to 12 minutes, until set and the bottoms are golden brown. Cool on a rack.

Ginger Cookies

Makes about 75 (2-inch) cookies, or 40 (3-inch) cookies

Using sour cream in these spiced cookies adds moisture and tang, and they happen to be excellent for making ice cream sandwiches. The dough is pretty sticky, so chilling it before scooping is essential, and using an ice cream scoop makes it easier to work with. My family loves them with homemade Vanilla Ice Cream (page 227), but try them with your favorite ice cream for an easy summer treat!

3 cups all-purpose flour

2 teaspoons baking soda

2 teaspoons ground ginger

1 teaspoon cinnamon

½ teaspoon kosher salt

¼ teaspoon cloves

2 cups sugar

1 cup (2 sticks) unsalted butter, softened

¾ cup sour cream

½ cup molasses

1 egg

Raw cane sugar for rolling

DIRECTIONS

1. Place the flour, baking soda, ginger, cinnamon, salt, and cloves in a medium bowl. Whisk to combine and set aside.

2. Place the sugar and butter in the bowl of a stand mixer fitted with the paddle attachment. Beat on medium-high until light and fluffy, about 2 minutes. Add the sour cream, molasses, and egg and beat until combined, scraping the bowl with a spatula as needed.

3. With the mixer on low, slowly add the flour mixture to the butter mixture. Remove the bowl from the mixer. Cover and chill for at least 30 minutes and up to 2 days.

4. Preheat oven to 350°F. Line two rimmed baking sheets with parchment paper.

5. Form the dough into 1 tablespoon-size balls. Roll in the cane sugar to coat and place 16 cookies on each baking sheet, evenly spaced apart. Bake until golden brown and crisp, 10 to 12 minutes. Cool on a rack. For 3-inch cookies, form into 2-tablespoon size balls and bake for 15 minutes.

Note

If making cookies for ice cream sandwiches, reduce the baking time by 1 to 2 minutes. This helps keep cookies soft when frozen.

Vanilla Ice Cream

Makes 2 quarts

My great-grandma Eleanor made this custard-style ice cream in a hand churner, and my mom has happy memories of cranking it on hot summer days when she was a teenager. These days, electric ice cream makers do most of the work, and you can have homemade ice cream in under an hour! The more egg yolks you add, the richer the custard will be. We love to serve this as a sweet end to a July dinner party, or to scoop onto chocolate chip or Ginger Cookies (page 224) for homemade ice cream sandwiches.

¾ cup sugar

2 tablespoons flour

½ teaspoon kosher salt

4 cups half-and-half

1 vanilla bean

2 to 4 egg yolks

DIRECTIONS

1. Combine the sugar, flour, and salt in a small saucepan. Whisk in 2 cups of the half-and-half. Scrape the seeds from the vanilla bean into the pan. Discard the pod or save it for homemade vanilla extract or vanilla sugar. Cook over medium heat until very thick and creamy, 4 to 5 minutes, whisking every minute or so. Do not boil—mixture will start to thicken when small bubbles form around the edge. Remove from the heat.

2. Whisk the egg yolks in a small bowl: 2 egg yolks, or up to 4 if you want richer ice cream. Add a little bit of the heated half-and-half mixture and whisk until combined. Slowly whisk the eggs into the half-and-half mixture. Cook over medium heat for 1 minute, whisking occasionally. Remove from the heat and refrigerate until chilled, at least 30 minutes and up to 1 day.

3. When chilled and ready to churn, whisk in the remaining half-and-half. Follow manufacturer's instructions to churn and freeze the ice cream. I like to freeze in 8-by-4-inch loaf pans for easy scooping, but quart-size plastic containers work well, too.

Variations

COFFEE ICE CREAM: *Add ¼ cup instant espresso powder and ½ teaspoon vanilla extract or paste instead of vanilla bean and seeds in step 1.*

BERRY ICE CREAM: *Make the vanilla ice cream as directed. While the ice cream base chills, combine 1 pound berries of your choice (strawberries, blackberries, blueberries, raspberries, and/or rhubarb), ¼ to ½ cup sugar, depending on the sweetness of your berries, and ¼ cup water in a large saucepan. Simmer for 15 minutes, until softened and bubbling. For a chunkier texture, layer the berry mixture into the churned ice cream in a swirling pattern and freeze. For a smoother syrup, blend the cooked berries and strain through a fine mesh sieve, then swirl into the churned ice cream and freeze.*

ACKNOWLEDGMENTS

There are so many people who are a part of this book. Needless to say, it would never have come to be without my grandmothers and great-grandmothers: Nancy, Veola, Eleanor, and Judith. Their recipes were the inspiration for everything in this book. I'm so grateful that they saved their recipes and for their talents and creativity in the kitchen.

To my agent, Leigh Eisenman: thank you for seeing the potential in an unknown author from the Midwest. Your belief in this idea from the beginning, your astute edits, and tireless work made it happen!

To the entire team at Countryman Press, including: Ann Treistman for her guidance and discerning edits, Allison Chi for her stunning design, Isabel McCarthy for her quick and responsive assistance, and Diane Durrett for her meticulous copyediting. Thank you for trusting my vision and turning this idea into a finished book. It's been an honor to work with each of you.

To my wonderful recipe testers: Abby Siegel, Amie DeHarpporte, Ariel Knutson, Blake Nelson, Brenda Siems, Bruce Wasser, Caragh Bartness, Chelsea Morse, Dave Michel, Diane Landis, Ellen Cushing, Ellie Barczak, Emily Lee, Emily Mitchell, Jayne William, Judy-Ann Ehrlich, Katie McCauley, Kimm Schneider, Kris Tostengard Michel, Kristen Ellingboe, Lauren Ryan, Leslie Levy, Linnea Campbell, Lynn Ellingboe, Manish Khettry, Mary Lindgren, Melissa Zink, Paula Oaks, Rebecca Maloney, Rosie Shoemaker Lynch, Sara Deforest, Selena Darrow, and Solveig Nelson. Your feedback was invaluable and helped make this a better book. That you volunteered your time to cook these recipes means so much to me.

To my photographer, Eliesa Johnson: your vision and talent is incredible. It was such a joy to collaborate with you on this project, and the images you shot brought such richness and depth to the book.

To my dear friends, Greta Cottington and Ariel Knutson: thank you for your advice, your expertise on Midwestern foods, your recipe feedback, and your friendship. Being able to ask for your opinion (or just a willing ear) throughout this process was priceless.

To my family, Mom, Dad, Solveig, Annelise, Blake, and Jake: thank you for being my taste-testers and proofreaders, for your honest feedback, for being willing models and photo assistants when I needed them, and for your constant support and excitement during every step of creating this book. I am so lucky to have you.

To Dashiell, who was with me every step of the way: this book is for you. To know who you are and where you come from. Your dad and I love you more than we can possibly say.

And to Ari: you tasted every recipe, did seemingly endless dishes, and have always been my greatest support and original cheerleader. I couldn't have done it without you. I love you.

INDEX